New Directions for
Child and Adolescent
Development

William Damon
EDITOR-IN-CHIEF

Reed W. Larson
Lene Arnett Jensen
INCOMING EDITORS-
IN-CHIEF

Changing Boundaries of Parental Authority During Adolescence

Judith Smetana
EDITOR

Number 108 • Summer 2005
Jossey-Bass
San Francisco

CHANGING BOUNDARIES OF PARENTAL AUTHORITY DURING ADOLESCENCE
Judith Smetana (ed.)
New Directions for Child and Adolescent Development, no. 108
William Damon, Editor-in-Chief

Microfilm copies of issues and articles are available in 16mm and 35mm, as well as microfiche in 105mm, through University Microfilms Inc., 300 North Zeeb Road, Ann Arbor, Michigan 48106-1346.

ISSN 1520-3247   electronic ISSN 1534-8687

NEW DIRECTIONS FOR CHILD AND ADOLESCENT DEVELOPMENT is part of The Jossey-Bass Education Series and is published quarterly by Wiley Subscription Services, Inc., a Wiley company, at Jossey-Bass, 989 Market Street, San Francisco, California 94103-1741. Periodicals postage paid at San Francisco, California, and at additional mailing offices. Postmaster: Send address changes to New Directions for Child and Adolescent Development, Jossey-Bass, 989 Market Street, San Francisco, CA 94103-1741.

New Directions for Child and Adolescent Development is indexed in Biosciences Information Service, Current Index to Journals in Education (ERIC), Psychological Abstracts, and Sociological Abstracts.

SUBSCRIPTIONS cost $90.00 for individuals and $205.00 for institutions, agencies, and libraries.

EDITORIAL CORRESPONDENCE should be sent to the Editor-in-Chief, William Damon, Stanford Center on Adolescence, Cypress Building C, Stanford University, Stanford, CA 94305.

Jossey-Bass Web address: www.josseybass.com

CONTENTS

Editor's Notes

Adolescence, and particularly early adolescence, is a period of rapid developmental change. The physical changes of puberty, new achievements due to cognitive development, and changes in adolescents' social status and social relationships all have been hypothesized to transform parent-adolescent relationships from more unilateral forms at the beginning of adolescence to more mutuality and greater autonomy, at least in some domains, by the end of adolescence. Thus, much research has focused on changes in the nature and quality of parent-adolescent relationships during adolescence.

In contrast, the implicit assumption of most of the research on parenting during adolescence is that parenting attitudes, beliefs, styles, and practices are relatively stable characteristics. Although there has been increasing appreciation of the reciprocal, bidirectional influences between parents and children (Collins and others, 2000), there has been surprisingly little attention to how parents adapt and alter their parenting strategies in response to the changing developmental needs of adolescents.

The chapters in this volume consider how parenting beliefs (including conceptions of parental authority, beliefs about parents' idealized control, and adolescents' obligations to obey parents) and parenting practices (including authoritative parenting, family rules, behavioral control, psychological control, and support) change during adolescence. The chapter authors conceptualize change in parenting in diverse ways. For instance, in Chapter One, Brian Barber, Suzanne Maughan, and Joseph Olsen examine longitudinal research following two cohorts of parents and adolescents for four years to consider whether different dimensions of parenting, including parental support, psychological control, and behavioral control, change over time. Their results suggest that stability, change, and fluctuating patterns all are characteristic of the adolescent period, depending on which dimension of parenting is examined. Thus, their research highlights where changes in parenting should be expected (or not) and the nature of that change.

The next three chapters consider variations in parenting according to the different realms of adolescents' experience. These chapters each consider how parenting shifts to accommodate changes in different domains of parental authority and control during adolescence and how differences in adolescents' and parents' perspectives on these issues potentially result in asynchronies and conflicts between parents and adolescents.

Chapter Two by Larry Nucci, Yuki Hasebe, and Maria Tereza Lins-Dyer uses the framework of social domain theory (Nucci, 1996; Smetana, 1995;

Turiel, 1983, 1998) to examine variations in parenting as a function of different social-cognitive domains (moral, conventional, prudential, personal, and overlapping). They propose that developmentally supportive parenting entails the provision of parental guidance and structure around children's moral, conventional, and prudential actions; parental permissiveness with regard to personal matters; and negotiation and flexibility over issues that entail intersections or overlaps between personal issues and matters of prudence, convention, or morality. Using research from several studies examining responses from children and adolescents in the United States, Japan, and Brazil, Nucci, Hasebe, and Lins-Dyer demonstrate that parental overcontrol of the personal domain is associated with adolescents' psychological symptoms.

Using data from a five-year longitudinal study of middle-class African American adolescents and their parents, Judith Smetana, Hugh Crean, and Nicole Campione-Barr in Chapter Three examine trajectories of change in African American adolescents' and mothers' conceptions of the legitimacy of parental authority in different domains. Like Barber, Maughan, and Olsen, Smetana and her colleagues find both stability (across the five years of study, adolescents and parents continued to affirm parents' legitimate authority to regulate moral and conventional issues) and change (from acceptance to greater rejection of parental authority to regulate prudential, personal, and multifaceted issues); they also find asynchronies between parents' and adolescents' beliefs, which lead to conflict in their relationships. Furthermore, like Nucci and his colleagues, Smetana, Crean, and Campione-Barr report that overcontrol of adolescents' personal freedoms leads to feelings of psychological control and that over time, changes in conceptions of legitimate parental authority influence adolescent adjustment.

In Chapter Four, Nancy Darling, Patricio Cumsille, and Liane Peña-Alampay examine cross-cultural variations in parenting beliefs and practices in relation to parenting styles and adolescent-parent conflict. They compare beliefs about legitimate parental authority and adolescents' obligations to obey parents in situations of conflict among Filipino, Chilean, and American youth. Their focus is on how responsible autonomy is negotiated in different domains and in different cultural contexts, and their findings indicate that the interrelationships among parenting styles, practices, beliefs, and parent-adolescent conflict vary in these three cultures. Their findings highlight the importance of considering the cultural context in understanding how responsible autonomy is achieved.

These chapters are followed by commentaries by Diana Baumrind, Laurence Steinberg, and Elliot Turiel. Each of these scholars provides integrative comments on the first four chapters and elaborate on the findings from their own perspectives. They draw attention to the paradigms structuring the different approaches and the consistencies and inconsistencies in associated constructs and measures. Their comments also highlight the novel contributions of this research, while outlining areas in need of further investigation. Thus, the chapters in this volume provide new directions for conceptualizing changes in parenting over the second decade of life and their implications for adolescent adjustment and well-being. The authors point to the need for developmentally sensitive models of parenting during adolescence that consider changes within domains over time and their influence on adolescent development and functioning.

Judith G. Smetana
Editor

References

Collins, W. A., and others. "Contemporary Research on Parenting: The Case for Nature and Nurture." *American Psychologist,* 2000, *55,* 218–232.

Nucci, L. P. "Morality and Personal Freedom." In E. S. Reed, E. Turiel, and T. Brown (eds.), *Values and Knowledge.* Mahwah, N.J.: Erlbaum, 1996.

Smetana, J. G. "Morality in Context: Abstractions, Ambiguities, and Applications." In R. Vasta (ed.), *Annals of Child Development.* London: Jessica Kingsley Publishers, 1995.

Turiel, E. *The Development of Social Knowledge: Morality and Convention.* Cambridge: Cambridge University Press, 1983.

Turiel, E. "Moral Development." In W. Damon (ed.), *Handbook of Child Psychology.* Vol. 3: N. Eisenberg (ed.), *Social, Emotional, and Personality Development.* (5th ed.) New York: Wiley, 1998.

JUDITH SMETANA is professor of psychology and pediatrics and director of the developmental psychology program at the University of Rochester, Rochester, New York.

1

Patterns of change in parental support, behavioral control, and psychological control were examined longitudinally across adolescence.

Patterns of Parenting Across Adolescence

Brian K. Barber, Suzanne L. Maughan, Joseph A. Olsen

The parent-adolescent relationship has received considerable attention throughout the twentieth century because of developmental changes that occur in both children and parents during this period. Different renditions of the nature of the parent-adolescent relationship have been offered. These range from the classic storm and stress characterizations to the currently popular, more modest estimates of "transformations" (Baumrind, 1991)— but all posit change.

Some research on change has assessed the quality of the relationship between parents and adolescents (for example, the level of closeness or conflict), grounding the work in psychoanalytic, sociobiological, or cognitive-developmental theories (Blos, 1979; Laursen and Collins, 1988; Smetana, 1988; Steinberg, 1989). Empirical evidence is mixed, depending in part on whether the focal aspects of the relationship are time spent together, types of conflicts, or levels of closeness. Conger and Ge (1999) suggest that much of this inconsistency is due to methodological problems in the mix of studies, and they offer their own findings of gradual increases in conflict/hostility and decrease in cohesion/warmth/supportiveness.

An approach to examine change in the parent-child relationship during adolescence that has received less consistent attention has been the

This study was supported by a FIRST Award grant from the National Institute of Mental Health (R29-MH47067–03) to Brian K. Barber. Appreciation is expressed to the administrators, teachers, and families of the Ogden Utah City School District for participating in this study.

investigation of the degree to which actual parenting behavior (for example, behavioral practices or styles parents use in interaction with their children) changes during adolescence. Although parents' behavior toward their adolescent children certainly is a factor in the overall quality of the relationship between parents and adolescents, it is not synonymous with it.

Parental Support, Behavioral Control, and Psychological Control

One recent trend in the study of parenting behaviors has been to revive and refine a tripartite classification of child- and parent-reported parenting behavior (Steinberg, Dornbusch, and Brown, 1992) first popularized by Schaefer (1965): acceptance/rejection, psychological control/psychological autonomy, and firm control/lax control. This tripartite organization of key parenting behaviors is also consistent with the basic components of classic parenting typologies (Baumrind, 1971, 1991; Steinberg and others, 1994).

Although some studies have assessed these parenting dimensions at multiple time points, most have focused on differential prediction of child and adolescent functioning over time and have not attempted a systematic assessment of the stability or change in these parenting dimensions across the developmental markers of adolescence. Other studies have assessed parenting behaviors quite similar to those included in Schaefer's model, but have been limited to the study of preadolescents or by small sample sizes. The purpose of the study described in this chapter was to provide an initial assessment of the three parenting dimensions across adolescence. It did so by testing mother, father, and adolescent reports of the three parenting dimensions in two cohorts (each approximately 350 families), each assessed over four consecutive years that cover the developmental markers of puberty and school transitions (cohort 1: ages eleven to thirteen; cohort 2: ages fourteen to seventeen). To further specify and validate change patterns, we analyzed both linear and nonlinear trends and also conducted trend interactions with sample characteristics of age of youth, sex of youth, social class, family structure, ethnicity, and religious affiliation.

As others have done, we use somewhat different labels for these parenting dimensions than did Schaefer (1965). We use the label *parental support* because Schaefer's acceptance construct appears to be just one of several parallel conceptualizations (for example, nurturance, warmth, affection) of a broader construct of perceived parental behaviors that, individually and collectively, support child and adolescent psychosocial development (Rollins and Thomas, 1979). We use *parental behavioral control* and *psychological control* because these labels better communicate the meaningful distinction between parent control of child or adolescent behavior and parental control of the child's or adolescent's psychological world apparent in Schaefer's original work (1965) and in more recent work (Barber, 1996, 2002; Gray and Steinberg, 1999). Parental behavioral control refers to parental behaviors that are intended to regulate children's behaviors to accord with prevailing family or social norms (Barber, 1996). Parental psychological control refers to parental behaviors that are nonresponsive to the emotional and psychological needs of children and stifle independent expression and autonomy (Barber, 2002; Schaefer, 1965).

For this study, we included two additional measures. Physical affection expressed by parents to their adolescents was included as an assessment of parental support (in addition to parental acceptance) in order to facilitate a direct comparison to past studies that have assessed change over time in this aspect of support. Limit setting was employed as an assessment of behavioral control (in addition to parental knowledge/monitoring) because of the recent concern raised about the adequacy of the common measure of parental monitoring as an indicator of parental control (Stattin and Kerr, 2000).

Despite variations in methodology, some studies set a relevant foundation for this study, given their focus on indexes of specific parenting behaviors similar to those used here. We have drawn on these studies to outline some tentative expectations as to stability or change in parental support, behavioral control, and psychological control.

Specifically, in studying parental support, Roberts and others (1984) and McNally and others (1991) found evidence that support a tentative expectation of declining levels of physical affection expressed by parents across adolescence. For items reflecting nonphysical supportive behavior, however, findings were mixed among stability, increases, and decreases for both mothers' and fathers' behaviors. Thus, there is not a solid basis to guide any clear expectations about change in nonphysical support.

In examining behavioral control, both McNally, Eisenberg, and Harris (1991) and Roberts, Block, and Block (1984) found no change over time in a single item assessing parental knowledge of their children's behavior, while in a study focused explicitly on the parental knowledge/monitoring construct, Laird, Pettit, Bates, and Dodge (2003) found that males reported decreases across adolescence. As for the setting of rules, Roberts and others (1984) found no change in a single item on rules, while McNally, Eisenberg, and Harris (1991), using the same item but aggregated as part of a larger control construct, found a linear increase across adolescence. It appears that there is some reason to expect that parental knowledge of their children's behavior might decrease across adolescence, but there is not enough evidence to advance any hypotheses about changes in rules or limits that parents set.

As for items representing parental psychological control, both Roberts, Block, and Block (1984) and McNally, Eisenberg, and Harris (1991) found patterns of either stability or increases in psychological control, but not decreases, across time. These findings, coupled with assertions that parental psychological control is driven by complexities in the lives of parents (such as their own parenting history, beliefs about parental authority, or their own psychological deficits; Barber, Bean, and Erickson, 2002), lead us to expect no declines in psychological control across adolescence.

In sum, although there have been some findings of change, the literatures that have investigated specific parental behaviors (with items conceptually similar to those used in this study) show either mixed patterns of change or little, if any, change. Indeed, both McNally, Eisenberg, and Harris (1991) and Roberts, Block, and Block (1984) concluded that the degree of continuity and stability over time was strong enough to imply that instead of altering their parenting practices in response to developmental changes, parents may behave toward children according to personal orientations toward child rearing that are based in beliefs, values, and philosophies that remain relatively stable across the development of the child and even despite significant changes in family formations (such as parental marital intactness). Consistent with this interpretation, Pettit and Laird (2002) have suggested that parenting behavior toward adolescents (specifically, psychological and behavioral control) is variously affected by parenting philosophy (as well as by parent personality, parents' own child rearing, and individual characteristics of children that are stable through adolescence). These notions of stable orientations toward child rearing are consonant with a social relations theoretical model that would predict more continuity than change in parent-child relations over time, resulting from the inherent stability of close relationships (and presumably the behaviors that reflect them) (Conger and Ge, 1999; Laursen and Collins, 1988).

Sample

Data came from the Ogden Youth and Family Project, a longitudinal study of families with adolescents in Ogden, Utah. The baseline sample was a random sample of fifth- and eighth-grade classrooms in the Ogden City School District in 1994. It consisted of 933 families with adolescent children. The sample was split equally between male and female students and grade, and was 71 percent white (16 percent Hispanic), 84 percent middle income, and 46 percent Mormon. In the first year, an extensive self-report survey of family interaction, personality, youth behavior, and peer, school, and neighborhood experiences was administered to the students in classrooms. Subsequent waves of the survey were done by multiple mailings to the students' homes. Both fifth- and eighth-grade cohorts were followed for four subsequent years, until 1997. The younger cohort was surveyed an additional time in 1998. The participation rate in the first year (in-class assessment) was over 90 percent. No follow-up was done of absentees. Multiple mailings following standard mail survey methodology (Dillman, 1978) were employed to maximize response rates in the subsequent years of data collection. Response rates were high: 78 to 80 percent for the different assessments. Details on sample sizes and composition in all years can be found in Barber, Stolz, Olsen, and Maughan (forthcoming). Analyses revealed that respondents and nonrespondents differed significantly only by way of a higher percentage of Mormons represented among the respondents.

Measures

This study employed multiple measures of the three relevant parenting dimensions: parental support, parental behavioral control, and parental psychological control.

Parental Support. Two forms of parental support were assessed in this study: acceptance and physical affection.

Acceptance. Parental acceptance was measured using the ten-item acceptance subscale from the thirty-item version of the Child Report of Parent Behavior Index (CRPBI) (Schaefer, 1965; E. Schludermann and S. Schludermann, personal communication, March 1988). Adolescents responded on a three-point Likert-type scale from 1 (*not like her or him*) to 3 (*a lot like her or him*) as to how well items described their mothers and fathers. Sample items are:

> My mother or father is a person who:

1. Makes me feel better after talking over my worries with her/him.
2. Smiles at me very often.
3. Enjoys doing things with me.

Parents responded to the equivalent items with appropriate changes made to each question. An equivalent three-point response scale also paralleled the youth response scale. Acceptable reliability was obtained for all measures.

Physical Affection. Physical affection was measured using two items: "My Mother/Father is a person who hugs me often" and "My Mother/Father is a person who kisses me often" (Barber and Thomas, 1986). The same three-point response scale as used for parental acceptance was used here. The parent versions of these same questions and response scales were employed to assess mother and father perspectives of their parent-child physical affection. Acceptable internal consistencies were obtained for both adolescents' ratings of mothers and fathers and parents' ratings of their own behavior.

Parental Behavioral Control. Two forms of parental behavioral control were assessed in this study: knowledge/monitoring and limit setting.

Parental Knowledge/Monitoring of Child Activities. Parental knowledge/monitoring was assessed with a five-item scale often used in research assessing self-reports of the parent-adolescent relationship (Brown, Mounts, Lamborn, and Steinberg, 1993). Scales using items such as these have been found to be particularly reliable and powerful indexes of family management and regulation (Patterson and Stouthamer-Loeber, 1984). The shift in the traditional label, monitoring, to include parental knowledge made here is in response to recent, valid criticisms that the measure is better described as parental awareness or knowledge of adolescent activities rather than the actual monitoring of those activities by parents such knowledge is presumed, in part, to be derived from (Stattin and Kerr, 2000). Students were asked the following questions separately for their father and mother:

How much does your father or mother *really* know about:

1. Where you go at night
2. Where you are most afternoons after school
3. How you spend your money
4. What you do with your free time
5. Who your friends are

Responses ranged from 1 (*doesn't know*) to 3 (*knows a lot*). The measures showed acceptable internal consistencies across the period of the study.

Parental Limit Setting. Parental limit setting was assessed with four items that measured adolescent reports of their parents' limit setting in the school context. Items were not differentiated by sex of parent. Adolescents responded on a four-point scale from 1 (*never*) to 4 (*often*) as to how often their parents performed these limit-setting behaviors during the past thirty days. Items were:

1. Restrict the amount of time you could watch television.
2. Check to see whether your homework was done.
3. Go over homework with you.
4. Check papers you brought home that a teacher had graded.

Equivalent questions and response scales for limit setting were answered by mothers and fathers. The measures showed acceptable internal consistencies across the period of the study.

Parental Psychological Control. Parental psychological control was measured by the eight-item Psychological Control Scale–Youth Self-Report (Barber, 1996). Participants responded on a three-point Likert-type scale from 1 (*not like her or him*) to 3 (*a lot like her or him*) as to how well items described their mothers and fathers. Sample items are:

My mother or father is a person who:

1. Is always trying to change how I feel or think about things.
2. Changes the subject whenever I have something to say.
3. Will avoid looking at me when I have disappointed her/him.

Mothers and fathers responded to the same (reworded) eight items according to the same (reworded response scale). The measures showed acceptable internal consistencies across the period of the study.

Plan of Analysis

The analysis plan consisted of repeated-measures analyses of variance with time (year of assessment) as the one within-subjects factor. Six between-subject factors representing the major demographic breaks in the sample were also considered. Specifically, we assessed within-subject interactions with time for each of the between-subjects variables: cohort (younger versus older), sex (male versus female), socioeconomic status (poor versus not poor), race (white versus nonwhite), religious affiliation (Mormon versus non-Mormon), and family structure (intact versus nonintact). Socioeconomic status was measured with one item: "Compared to other kids your age, how well-off do you think your family is?" (Pearlin, Lieberman, Meneghan, and Mullan, 1981). Responses ranged from 1 (*We are a lot poorer than most*) to 5 (*We are a lot richer than most*). This scale was dichotomized, with responses of 1 and 2 coded 1 (*poor*) and all other responses coded 2 (*not poor*). This produced a percentage of poor (13 percent) that matches the percentage of families that live under the poverty line in Ogden, Utah, based on census information from 1989 (Slater and Hall, 1996; U.S. Bureau of the Census, 1996).

Results

Following are the results for the analyses of all measures of parental support, behavioral control, and psychological control.

Parental Support. Two measures of parental support were analyzed: parental acceptance and parental physical affection.

Parental Acceptance. Generally parental acceptance remained stable across time. This was true for youth reports of their mothers' acceptance and for fathers' reports of their own acceptance, for both of which no significant change was detected. Although there was a significant quadratic change effect for mothers' reports of their own acceptance, the drop in mean level from 1994 to 1995 (2.60 to 2.55) was recovered by 1997 (2.61) to reach the 1994 level; thus, over the full span of the study, mothers' reported acceptance stayed relatively constant as well. These patterns held regardless of sex, age, economic well-being, family structure, and religious affiliation of the adolescent. These findings of general stability of parental acceptance are consistent with those of McNally, Eisenberg, and Harris (1991).

Youth reported a significant decline in acceptance from their fathers. The effect was linear, although constant from year 3 to year 4 (yearly means: 2.33, 2.29, 2.25, 2.25). There was also a significant interaction between time and economic well-being, whereby poorer youth reported an initial increase and subsequent decrease of father acceptance. The reverse pattern, an initial decrease followed by some increase in father acceptance, was reported by less poor youth.

Parental Physical Affection. There was a clear pattern of decreased physical affection linearly across the four years of the study. This was the case for youth reports of both parents (yearly means for mothers: 2.31, 2.28, 2.24, 2.20; yearly means for fathers: 2.08, 1.94, 1.87, 1.84) and father reports of their own physical affection toward their adolescents (yearly means: 2.27, 2.08, NA, 1.95). Although not statistically significant, yearly means also declined linearly for mother reports of their own physical affection (2.50,

2.41, NA, 2.38). These patterns held regardless of sex, age, economic well-being, family structure, and religious affiliation of the adolescent. This pattern of decline is consistent with both Roberts, Block, and Block (1984) and McNally, Eisenberg, and Harris (1991).

Parental Behavioral Control. Two measures of parental behavioral control were analyzed: parental knowledge/monitoring and parental limit setting.

Knowledge/Monitoring. There was a reporter-based difference in patterns of change in parental knowledge/monitoring of their adolescents' activities. Youth reported stability in monitoring from both parents, although youth reports of mothers' knowledge/monitoring did increase in the second year and then returned to the first-year level for the following two assessments (year means: 2.53, 2.57, 2.54, 2.53). This pattern was constant regardless of sex, age, economic well-being, family structure, and religious affiliation of the adolescent. Both parents, however, reported linear declines over the course of the study in their knowledge/monitoring of their adolescents' activities (yearly means for mothers: 2.84, 2.81, NA, 2.73; yearly means for fathers: 2.72, 2.68, NA, 2.56). The decline in father-reported knowledge/monitoring was also qualified by race, whereby fathers of white youth reported steady knowledge/monitoring through year 2 followed by a linear decline. Fathers of nonwhite youth reported a steeper decline between the first two assessments, followed by a slower decline thereafter.

Limit Setting. There was a consistent linear decline in reports of parental limit setting. This pattern held for youth reports of parents (yearly means: NA, 2.64, 2.54, 2.43) and parent reports (yearly means for mothers: 3.24, 3.04, NA, 2.43; yearly means for fathers: 2.99, 2.73, NA, 2.54). This pattern of decline did not vary by demographic characteristics, with the one exception that mothers of youth from nonintact families reported a steeper decline in limit setting than did mothers of youth from intact families.

This finding of decreased control in the form of rules for schoolwork is consistent with theoretical positions positing declining parental control during adolescence, but it is not supportive of Roberts, Block, and Block's finding (1984) of stability in a single item measuring rules or McNally, Eisenberg, and Harris's finding (1991) of an increase in an aggregated control construct that included the same item on rules.

Parental Psychological Control. There was a consistent pattern of change in reports of psychological control, whereby decreased psychological control was reported in the second year, followed by a rise over the third year (fourth year for parent reports). This was true for reports by mothers (yearly means: 1.49, 1.28, NA, 1.36), by fathers (yearly means: 1.51, 1.29, NA, 1.37), and for youth reports of fathers (yearly means: 1.49, 1.45, 1.50, 1.51). Although there was no significant change in youth reports of mothers' psychological control, the annual means did accord with this same pattern (1.49, 1.44, 1.45, 1.50). One qualification of the general quadratic pattern is that youth reports of psychological control of both parents in the final year of the study returned to or exceeded the first-year levels, whereas parental reports were lower in the last year compared to the first year. These patterns also held regardless of sex, age, economic well-being, family structure, and religious affiliation of the adolescent.

Discussion

Although changes in the relations between parents and their children during adolescence have been a frequent topic of interest to lay, professional, and academic circles, the actual empirical evidence for change has not been particularly strong or consistent. Whereas most studies have focused on change in the general quality of the relationship (how much conflict or closeness is felt between the parties), this study emphasized parenting behavioral practices, focusing on three central dimensions of parenting behavior that have been studied systematically, both historically and currently.

The study was limited by using a regional sample (Rocky Mountain) and by exclusive reliance on self-reported parenting. It will be important to validate the findings of this study using other samples and different methods for assessing parental behaviors. Nevertheless, the study tested carefully for variations within the sample to assess how generalizable patterns of findings were for gender, age, social class, ethnic, family structure, and religious groups represented in the sample. Having multiple individuals from the same family reporting on the same indexes of parenting also helped to validate the findings. A further advantage of the study is that it included four annual assessments (three for parent reports) of perceived parenting practices among two cohorts, whose experiences during that four-year period included pubertal development and the transition to middle school and high school.

Depending on the parenting variable in question, the findings of this study revealed both stability and change. Before discussing these findings, it is noteworthy that there was substantial consistency in the observed patterns across reporter and sample subgroup, a consistency that helps validate the findings. Thus, for example, with one exception (parental knowledge/monitoring), the same patterns of change or stability were generally found regardless of whether youth-, mother-, or father-reported data were analyzed. Also, patterns of stability or change did not vary across most of the sample subgroups; patterns were the same for males and females, younger and older adolescents, Mormons and non-Mormons, and adolescents from single- and dual-parent families. There were only two cases in which sample subgroups had varied patterns, and both were for fathers. That nonwhite adolescents reported a steeper decline in father knowledge/monitoring than did white adolescents and that poorer adolescents reported a reversed pattern of increased and then decreased father acceptance than did adolescents who were less poor are interesting findings. However, they are unique enough in these analyses to require validation with other data sets with better distributions and measures of ethnicity and social class before they could be adequately interpreted.

The clearest patterns of change in the findings of this study occurred for the two most behaviorally specific measures, physical affection and limit setting: both were reported to have declined significantly across adolescence. The decline in physically expressed parental support is sensible given that in the United States, notions of physical intimacy and gender socialization typically reserve hugging and kissing for younger children. Contrary to this pattern (except for youth reports of their fathers), there was relative stability across adolescence in reported parental acceptance. This pattern is also not surprising when considering that by adolescence, parents have likely already established a pattern or behavioral style of basic support to their children that should not be expected to fluctuate substantially during adolescence. This is particularly so given the rather macro-level format of the assessment, that is, yearly reports of the degree to which a set of behaviors describes parents.

As for behavioral control, the decline in limit setting is sensible given the tendency of parents to begin to reduce, or at least alter, some of the specific limits they set as they attempt to grant legitimate autonomy to their adolescents. That only parents reported declines in the less behaviorally specific form of behavioral control (knowledge/monitoring) raises interesting questions that should be investigated thoroughly in data sets (unlike our own) in which better determinations of the source of parental knowledge can be made (Stattin and Kerr, 2000). To the extent that this commonly used measure is a legitimate assessment of parental control (monitoring behaviors are responsible, at least in part, for the knowledge), then the discrepancy between parent-reported decline and adolescent-reported stability in control is quite interesting. Perhaps some adolescents, overly sensitive to any control, might not adequately note the decreases in the control that parents report. To the extent that parental knowledge stems not primarily from monitoring behaviors but from adolescent disclosure to parents of their activities, the discrepancy is again interesting. Perhaps, given increasing exercise of autonomy in some realms, parents fear that their adolescents are not telling them all, or as much as they did when younger.

Finally, as anticipated, there was no pattern of decline in parental use of psychological control. Instead, there was either stability or fluctuation across the four-year span of the study, with increases consistently following an initial decline in reported psychological control. Much less is known about the nature of parental psychological control than is of support or behavioral control, and thus we hesitate to interpret too much from this pattern. The initial decline is interesting, especially since both cohorts of adolescents underwent a school change in the second year. One speculation would be that parents noted the particular stress of this transition and relaxed their intrusive control, at least temporarily. Replication and more finely grained analyses would be necessary to confirm this or other speculations. But at least it can be concluded that in this sample, this particular type of control functioned quite differently from the two measures of behavioral control, for both of which there was complete or partial evidence for declining control across adolescence.

In sum, this test of more behaviorally oriented assessments of parenting showed no consistent evidence for the often theorized decline in relational functioning between parents and their adolescent children. Instead we found differences in change patterns depending on the specific dimensions of parenting in question, with general stability for nonphysical supportive behaviors, decline in physical affection, general decline for behavioral control (particularly for explicit rules), and a fluctuating pattern for psychological control.

References

Barber, B. K. "Parental Psychological Control: Revisiting a Neglected Construct." *Child Development,* 1996, *67,* 3296–3319.

Barber, B. K. (ed.). *Intrusive Parenting: How Psychological Control Affects Children and Adolescents.* Washington, D.C.: American Psychological Association Press, 2002.

Barber, B. K., Bean, R. L., and Erickson, L. D. "Expanding the Study and Understanding of Psychological Control." In B. K. Barber (ed.), *Intrusive Parenting: How Psychological Control Affects Children and Adolescents.* Washington, D.C.: American Psychological Association Press, 2002.

Barber, B. K., Stolz, H. E., Olsen, J. A., and Maughan, S. L. "Parental Support, Psychological Control, and Behavioral Control: Assessing Relevance Across Time, Method, and Culture." Forthcoming.

Barber, B. K., and Thomas, D. L. "Dimensions of Fathers' and Mothers' Supportive Behavior: The Case for Physical Affection." *Journal of Marriage and Family,* 1986, *48,* 783–794.

Baumrind, D. "Current Patterns of Parental Authority." *Developmental Psychology Monographs,* 1971, *4*(1, part 2), 1–102.

Baumrind, D. "The Influence of Parenting Style on Adolescent Competence and Substance Use." *Journal of Early Adolescence,* 1991, *11,* 56–95.

Blos, P. *The Adolescent Passage.* Guilford, Conn.: International Universities Press, 1979.

Brown, B. B., Mounts, N., Lamborn, S. D., and Steinberg, L. "Parenting Practices and Peer Group Affiliation in Adolescence." *Child Development,* 1993, *63,* 391–400.

Conger, R. D., and Ge, X. "Conflict and Cohesion in Parent-Adolescent Relations: Changes in Emotional Expression from Early to Mid Adolescence." In M. J. Cox and J. Brooks-Gunn (eds.), *Conflict and Cohesion in Families: Causes and Consequences.* Mahwah, N.J.: Erlbaum, 1999.

Dillman, D. A. *Mail and Telephone Surveys: The Total Design Method.* New York: Wiley, 1978.

Gray, M. R., and Steinberg, L. "Unpacking Authoritative Parenting: Reassessing a Multidimensional Construct." *Journal of Marriage and the Family,* 1999, *61,* 574–587.

Laird, R. D., Pettit, G. S., Bates, J. E., and Dodge, K. A. "Parents' Monitoring-Relevant Knowledge and Adolescents' Delinquent Behavior: Evidence of Correlated Developmental Changes and Reciprocal Influences." *Child Development,* 2003, *74*(3), 752–768.

Laursen, B., and Collins, W. A. "Conceptual Changes During Adolescence and Effects upon Parent-Child Relationships." *Journal of Adolescent Research,* 1988, *3,* 119–139.

McNally, S., Eisenberg, N., and Harris, J. D. "Consistency and Change in Maternal Child-Rearing Practices: A Longitudinal Study." *Child Development,* 1991, *62,* 190–198.

Patterson, G. R., and Stouthamer-Loeber, M. "The Correlation of Family Management Practices and Delinquency." *Child Development,* 1984, *55,* 1299–1307.

Pearlin, L. I., Lieberman, M. A., Meneghan, E. G., and Mullan, J. T. "The Stress Process." *Journal of Health and Social Behavior,* 1981, *22,* 337–356.

Pettit, G. S., and Laird, R. "Psychological Control and Monitoring in Early Adolescence: The Role of Parental Involvement and Earlier Child Adjustment." In B. K. Barber (ed.), *Intrusive Parenting: How Psychological Control Affects Children and Adolescents.* Washington, D.C.: American Psychological Association, 2002.

Roberts, G. C., Block, J. H., and Block, J. "Continuity and Change in Parents' Child-Rearing Practices." *Child Development,* 1984, *55,* 586–597.

Rollins, B. C., and Thomas, D. L. "Parental Support, Power, and Control Techniques in the Socialization of Children." In W. R. Burr, R. Hill, F. I. Nye, and I. L. Reiss (eds.), *Contemporary Theories About the Family.* Vol. 1: *Research Based Theories.* New York: Free Press, 1979.

Schaefer, E. W. "Children's Reports of Parental Behavior: An Inventory." *Child Development,* 1965, *36,* 413–424.

Silverberg, S. B., and Steinberg, L. "Adolescent Autonomy, Parent-Adolescent Conflict, and Parental Well-Being." *Journal of Youth and Adolescence,* 1987, *16,* 293–312.

Slater, C. M., and Hall, G. E. (eds.). *County and City Extra Annual Metro City and County Data Book.* Lanham, Md.: Bernan, 1996.

Smetana, J. G. "Adolescents' and Parents' Conceptions of Parental Authority." *Child Development,* 1988, *59,* 321–335.

Stattin, H., and Kerr, M. "Parental Monitoring: A Reinterpretation." *Child Development,* 2000, *71,* 1072–1085.

Steinberg, L. "Pubertal Maturation and Parent-Adolescent Distance: An Evolutionary Perspective." In G. R. Adams, R. Montemayor, and T. P. Gulotta (eds.), *Biology of Adolescent Behavior and Development.* Thousand Oaks, Calif.: Sage, 1989.

Steinberg, L., Dornbusch, S. M., and Brown, B. B. "Ethnic Differences in Adolescent Achievement." *American Psychologist,* 1992, *47,* 723–729.

Steinberg, L., and others. "Over-Time Changes in Adjustment and Competence Among Adolescents from Authoritative, Authoritarian, Indulgent, and Neglectful Families." *Child Development,* 1994, *65,* 754–770.

U.S. Bureau of the Census. *County and City Data Books.* Washington, D.C.: U.S. Government Printing Office, 1996.

BRIAN K. BARBER *is professor of child and family studies at the University of Tennessee at Knoxville.*

SUZANNE L. MAUGHAN *is assistant professor of sociology at the University of Nebraska at Kearney.*

JOSEPH A. OLSEN *is associate professor of sociology at Brigham Young University in Provo, Utah.*

2

The psychological consequences of parental control over adolescents' issues of privacy and personal choice are explored with youth from varying cultural backgrounds.

Adolescent Psychological Well-Being and Parental Control of the Personal

Larry Nucci, Yuki Hasebe, Maria Tereza Lins-Dyer

There is a considerable body of evidence that an authoritative parenting style (Baumrind, 1971) in which parental control is tempered with a willingness to negotiate with the child promotes psychological adjustment (Lamborn, Mounts, Steinberg, and Dornbusch, 1991; Steinberg, Lamborn, Darling, Mounts, and Dornbusch, 1994). Most of the existing literature, however, treats parenting style as a unitary construct. Thus, it is unclear from this global characterization as to whether parents should negotiate with their children around all issues or remain firm on some and be more flexible around others. This chapter reports on a series of studies that have made use of more recent work in which depictions of parenting have been refined to provide a theory-based distinction among aspects of children's conduct that parents should legitimately regulate, as opposed to those behaviors that should be subject to negotiation or given over to the child to determine (Smetana, 1995; Smetana and Daddis, 2002). This latter work has drawn from social cognitive domain theory distinctions among moral, conventional, and personal areas of conduct (Turiel, 1998). The studies discussed in this chapter have used these domain distinctions to explore the impact that perceived parental control over personal domain issues has on the psychological well-being of adolescents.

Prior work employing domain theory has demonstrated that both children and parents view moral actions that impinge on the rights and welfare of others as legitimately subject to parental authority (Smetana, 1995; Tisak and Tisak, 1990). Consistent with those findings, studies of adolescent-parent conflict have shown that moral issues are rarely the

NEW DIRECTIONS FOR CHILD AND ADOLESCENT DEVELOPMENT, no. 108, Summer 2005   © Wiley Periodicals, Inc.

subject of disputes between parents and their adolescents (Smetana, 1989; Smetana and Asquith, 1994; Smetana and Gaines, 1999). Similarly, adolescents and parents tend to view parental control as legitimate when it is exerted over children's actions that have prudential consequences for the health and safety of the child or pertain to the general conventions of society (Smetana, 1989, 1995; Smetana and Asquith, 1994; Smetana and Gaines, 1999; Tisak and Tisak, 1990).

In contrast with this acceptance of parental authority, children tend to reject the notion that parents should regulate behaviors that fall within what has been termed the personal domain (Nucci, 1981, 1996). The personal refers to actions that comprise the private aspects of one's life, such as the contents of a diary and issues that are matters of preference and choice (such as friends, music, and hairstyle) rather than right or wrong. It has been proposed that the establishment of control over the personal domain emerges from the need to establish boundaries between the self and others and is critical to the establishment of personal autonomy and individual identity (Nucci, 1996). For this reason, most instances of children's resistance to parental authority are thought to reflect these underlying psychological strivings rather than a more generalized resistance to parental authority (Nucci, 1996, 2001).

On the basis of this more recent work, one might expect that developmentally supportive parenting would entail the provision of parental guidance and structure around children's actions entailing moral, prudential, and conventional issues. Or parental permissiveness might be the more appropriate response with respect to children's activities that comprise personal matters. Finally, negotiation and flexibility would appear to be the more appropriate parental stance with respect to issues that intersect or overlap between the personal and matters of prudence, convention, or morality. This more differentiated view of parenting is consistent with research indicating that as opposed to permissive and authoritarian parenting styles, authoritative parenting is characterized by the tendency to distinguish among their children's actions by domain and coordinate their own tendencies to regulate their adolescent children's behavior by domain (Smetana, 1995). What characterized authoritative parents within this particular sample was their tendency to exert control over multifaceted issues that intersect the personal with matters of convention and prudence and to be permissive with respect to personal domain issues (Smetana, 1995). However, within the group of parents classified as authoritative, variance in tendencies of parents to grant personal jurisdiction over multifaceted issues was found to predict adolescent autonomy development (Smetana, 1995). Thus, the predictive power of associations between parenting and healthy child outcomes was enhanced by awareness of approaches to control over actions within domains beyond what was afforded by information about parenting style (Smetana, 1995).

Smetana (1995) highlights the importance of attending to differences in parental tendencies to afford adolescents personal jurisdiction over actions that comprise personal matters. Because the definition of what is personal is bound up with collective definitions of conventional regulation as well as an inherent overlap between issues of the child's safety and the child's sense of personal ownership of his or her own body, some degree of conflict between children and parents over the child's conduct is inevitable (see Smetana, 2002, for a comprehensive summary of research on this issue). These conflicts are evident in early childhood (Nucci and Weber, 1995) and expand as children enter adolescence and lay claim to greater areas of personal control (Smetana, 1989; Smetana and Asquith, 1994; Smetana and Gaines, 1999). The question explored in this chapter is whether the dynamic between parental authority and adolescent claims to an area of privacy and discretion is related to adolescent psychological adjustment.

This position suggests that when parental efforts to control adolescent behavior move beyond healthy monitoring and guidance into intrusive efforts to manage issues and behaviors within the personal and private areas of their children's lives, such control amounts to what Steinberg (1990) and Barber (Barber and Harmon, 2002) refer to as psychological control. Parental engagement in psychological control is thought to interfere with adolescents' development of a sense of independence, identity, and personal integrity (Barber and Harmon, 2002). In concert with this proposal are findings reported by Smetana and Daddis (2002) that adolescents who believed that parents should have less legitimate control over what the authors described as ambiguously personal acts and who viewed their parents as exerting more restrictive control over these acts also rated their mothers as more psychologically controlling. (A detailed discussion of this research is contained in Chapter Three, this volume.)

In addition to exploring the general hypothesis that parental overcontrol of the personal domain is linked to adolescent psychological maladjustment, the research presented in this chapter took some preliminary steps at examining whether that association is limited to children raised within Western culture, or if this adolescent-parent dynamic reflects more general factors of psychological development that extend to presumably collectivist cultural settings. Because the degree of parental control is often associated with social class, the research presented built from prior work taking social class into account when exploring cultural effects. The impact of parental control was explored within two contexts. One study (Lins-Dyer, 2003) looked at the impact of parental overcontrol on Mexican American and Mexican immigrant adolescent students' academic performance in an urban school setting. The second study (Hasebe, Nucci, and Nucci, 2004) examined the impact of parental control on Japanese and American adolescents' self-reports of psychological symptoms.

Background Research

Prior cross-cultural studies of adolescents' and parents' concepts of the personal domains of children have indicated that the identification of children's and adolescents' areas of privacy and prerogative are not limited to children and adults from individualistic cultures. These prior studies have included middle-class African Americans (Smetana and Gaines, 1999; Smetana and Daddis, 2002) and children and adults from northeastern Brazil (Nucci, Camino, and Milnitsky-Sapiro, 1996) and Hong Kong (Yau and Smetana, 2003). The results from two such studies from our research group will help to set the stage for this discussion.

The first study (Nucci, Camino, and Milnitsky-Sapiro, 1996) explored middle- and lower-class northeastern Brazilian children's and adolescents' judgments of whether the child protagonist rather than the parent should be able to control or determine the child's actions as depicted in a series of scenarios. Some of the scenarios presented actions about moral, prudential, or conventional issues, and others depicted actions fitting theoretical definitions of the personal domain. The findings regarding the personal domain issues are of interest for this discussion. The results were that middle-class Brazilian children as young as eight years of age tended to treat personal issues as within the child's discretionary authority and provided more autonomy, rights, and privacy justifications than authority and norm justifications for their judgments about personal issues. Eight-year-old lower-class children, in contrast, were more likely to state that the parent should control these same personal domain issues. These younger lower-class children also provided more authority and norm justifications than autonomy, rights, and privacy justifications in support of their evaluations of personal items. However, analyses of age effects indicated that for both social classes, there was an increasing tendency with age for children to claim control over personal issues. Consistent with these claims of greater control, both social classes of Brazilian children tended with age to provide more autonomy and rights justifications relative to authority and norms justifications in support of their judgments about personal domain items. By age sixteen, there were · no social class differences in the tendencies of young people to treat personal issues as matters that should be up to them rather than subject to regulation by external authority.

This study demonstrated that children and adolescents within a collectivist culture differentiated personal issues from matters of convention, morality, and prudence. Although social class had an impact on children's judgments of the legitimacy of parental authority over personal domain issues, this social class effect was itself modulated by the dynamics of children's development.

A recent unpublished follow-up study in the same region of northeastern Brazil (Lins-Dyer and Nucci, 2004) makes this point perhaps even more clearly. In this study, we compared the parental authority judgments of 126 middle-class and 126 lower-class girls with the judgments of their mothers regarding a series of forty-one hypothetical behaviors that fit within the conventional, personal, prudential, or overlapping domain categories as defined within domain theory. The girls ranged in age from twelve to sixteen years old.

We hypothesized that the views of our Brazilian sample would roughly map onto the domain-differentiated developmental pattern found in prior work with Brazilian and U.S. samples (Nucci, Camino, and Milnitsky-Sapiro, 1996). We also predicted on the basis of those earlier findings that the views maintained by the adolescent daughters regarding who should control their behavior would be similar across social classes, but that the lower-class mothers would be more likely than middle-class mothers to view themselves as exerting greater actual control. More specifically, we hypothesized that the social class discrepancy would be around issues of convention and prudence reflective of the mothers' concerns about the objectively greater social and personal risks that confront lower-class children and adolescents. This set of predictions about social class effects on the views of mothers was based on findings from prior studies (Kohn, 1969; Kohn and Schooler, 1983; Nucci and Milnitsky-Sapiro, 1995) indicating that working- and lower-class parents place greater emphasis on authority and parental control over their children than do middle-class parents. This is due to parental perceptions of the need for working-class children to learn to accommodate to the greater power of middle- and upper-class authority and to reduce their perceived greater vulnerability to street crime and other violence.

To elicit judgments of mothers and daughters in this study (Lins-Dyer and Nucci, 2004), we employed a questionnaire instrument, the Parental Authority Index (PAI), originally developed for use in a study with Japanese and U.S. adolescents (Hasebe, Nucci, and Nucci, 2004), which we describe in greater detail below. The PAI is similar in format to the Family Decision Making Checklist (Dornbusch and others, 1985) and Steinberg and Silverberg's Adolescent Autonomy Measure (1986). Unlike these measures, the PAI was designed to provide separate estimates of adolescents' judgments regarding parental control as a function of the domain of the actions in question. The PAI is composed of two sections that present participants with identical lists of behaviors they might engage in or decisions that they might make. In the first section of the measure, which comprises the Ideal Control Index (IC), participants are asked to indicate for each item who they think *should* make the decisions about a given topic. Respondents provide one of five responses ranging from, "I should be the one to decide this without having to discuss this with my parents," to "My parents and I should make this decision together," to "My parents should be able to decide/tell me what to do about this without discussing it with me." In the second section, the Perceived Control Index (PC), participants respond to the same items using a similar five-point scale. This time they evaluate each item in terms of who actually *would* make the decision (for example, "I would be the one to decide this without having to discuss this with my parents").

The forty-one items within the instrument have three scales: Personal Domain Scale (PDS), Prudential/Conventional Domain Scale (PCDS), and Overlapping Scale (ODS). Items were included within a given scale on the basis of their theoretical fit with the scale definition and the psychometric criteria discussed below. Initially the measure also included prototypical moral items. However, these elicited no variance in participants' responses (virtually all participants treated such issues as entirely within parental authority), and thus they were eliminated from the final version of the instrument. Consistent with prior research (Nucci, Camino, and Milnitsky-Sapiro, 1996; Smetana, 1989), preliminary analyses indicated that adolescents made similar judgments regarding parental control over prudential and conventional items, and these items were subsequently collapsed within a single (PCDS) scale. The resulting three scales corresponded to areas of adolescent conduct consistent with parental behavioral control (PCDS), negotiated parental control (ODS), and parental intrusion associated with psychological control (PDS). The latter two scales represented refinements of the Smetana and Daddis (2002) measure by separating prototypical personal items from those that are ambiguously within the personal domain.

Psychometric properties of the PAI were initially determined with a sample of 230 U.S. adolescents. All scales had excellent internal consistencies (alphas > .86). There were seven items in the U.S. version of the PDS of each index, seven in the PCDS; the third scale, the ODS, contained eighteen items involving mixed events that entailed an overlap between the personal and either social convention or prudence. A factor analysis including all forty-one items indicated that the two "prototypical domain" scales, the PDS and PCDS, were orthogonal to one another. As would be expected, items from the ODS loaded to some degree on either the PDS or PCDS scales. However, when the items of the ODS were analyzed separately, all loaded on a single factor.

The version of the PAI employed in northeastern Brazil (Lins-Dyer and Nucci, 2004) was translated into Portuguese by the first author, a native Brazilian. Some items were altered to fit the Brazilian setting. For example, the PCDS item "Whether to go outside in cold weather without a coat" was changed to "Whether to go to the beach without wearing sun block." The Cronbach alpha levels for the individual scales were somewhat lower than for the U.S. context, but still well within the acceptable range (.70–.81)

With respect to judgments of Idealized Control (Who should control the action?), we found the expected effects for domain and development. Across ages and social classes, personal issues were judged to be more legitimately subject to control by the daughter and prudential and conventional issues more legitimately subject to control by the mother, with overlapping issues intermediate in terms of who should exert control. There were no age or class effects on judgments about the control of personal issues. Across ages and social classes, daughters judged such issues as ones that should be subject to the daughters' discretion and control. With age, daughters indicated that overlapping issues and matters of convention and prudence should increasingly fall within their own rather than their mothers' jurisdiction. There were no social class effects for these judgments. Within the period of adolescence at least, Brazilian girls present very similar idealized views of who should determine or control decision making about their personal, prudential, and conventional areas of conduct. Not surprisingly, daughters' perceptions of who actually does control decision making about their behaviors resulted in judgments indicating that mothers were perceived as exerting greater control than the daughters would have ideally preferred.

Here we did observe a social class effect. Consistent with the earlier research with Brazilian participants (Nucci, Camino, and Milnitsky-Sapiro, 1996), lower-class girls perceived their mothers as exerting greater actual control over their actions than did middle-class girls. This was particularly the case with respect to prudential/conventional issues. The daughters' perceptions of their mothers' control patterns were mirrored in the mothers' own self-reports of their judgments about who should control their daughters' decision making about personal, prudential/conventional, and overlapping issues. As had been anticipated, the mothers provided differential patterns of control over their daughters as a function of the domain of the behaviors. Mothers reported exerting very little control over their daughters' personal issues, greater involvement in issues entailing overlap, and the greatest degree of control over conventions and actions entailing prudential risks to their daughters. The only social class difference was around matters of convention and prudence. Lower-class mothers reported exerting greater authority over their daughters' actions in these areas than did middle-class mothers.

The studies just discussed, along with a number of others (Nucci and Milnitsky-Sapiro, 1995; Smetana and Daddis, 2002; Smetana and Gaines, 1999, Yau and Smetana, 2003), have provided evidence that parental authority is neither perceived by adolescents and children nor applied by parents in a uniform fashion across the range of children's behaviors. On the contrary, considerable evidence now exists that parents across cultures and social classes differentiate between actions that are legitimately subject to parental authority and those private and personal actions and issues that parents and adolescents alike view as primarily within the child's area of privacy and discretion.

We now turn to a discussion of cross-cultural research that has investigated whether there are negative psychological consequences for children and adolescents whose parents extend their authority beyond guidance around issues of convention and personal safety into efforts to control areas of adolescent behavior that fall within the personal domain.

The Impact of Parental Overcontrol of the Personal Academic Performance

A number of studies have concluded that authoritative parenting is associated with academic achievement (Dornbusch and others, 1987; Steinberg, Mounts, Lamborn, and Dornbusch, 1991, 1992). In the work we discuss here, Lins-Dyer (2003) applied the distinctions afforded by domain theory to examine more specifically the relationship between parental control over children's behaviors and academic achievement. Participants in the study were 236 Mexican American and Mexican immigrant adolescents in grades 8 and 10 in public schools within a large midwestern city. The underlying hypothesis was that the impact of parental authority on students' school performance would not be due to the application of authority per se, but rather its application as a function of the child's activity domain. Control over issues of convention and prudence was expected to be positively associated with academic performance, while relative "overcontrol" of actions within the personal domain and overlapping issues would be associated with lower academic performance. Academic performance was estimated through students' self-reported grades and their self-assessments of how much they felt they were learning in school on a three-point scale from "little" to "very much." Perceptions of parental control were assessed through use of the PAI.

Lins-Dyer (2003) had anticipated that students who were new to the United States and members of immigrant households would report higher degrees of parental control for the prudential/conventional and domain overlapping issues than would Mexican Americans whose parents had been born and raised in the United States. Because immigrant status is generally confounded with social class, she obtained a separate estimate of Mexican-cultural involvement of her Mexican American sample (for example, trips to Mexico to visit relatives, family celebration of traditional holidays). She also obtained information regarding whether the Mexican American children were first- or later-generation residents of the United States. These initial background data revealed the expected patterns in which the adolescents of more traditional Mexican American and Mexican immigrant families reported greater degrees of parental control than did second- and later-generation, more acculturated Mexican American families. Within these broad trends, however, there were no differences in the self-reports of students from the Mexican American and Mexican immigrant backgrounds with respect to their Idealized conceptions of parental control over the personal domain. Also as expected, there was an age-related tendency for participants from both backgrounds to report less parental control over overlapping and prudential/conventional issues at grade 10 than at grade 8.

Parental Control and Self-Reported Learning in School. One estimate of the relationship between parental control and academic performance was students' reports of how much they perceived themselves to be learning in school on a three-point scale from "little" to "very much." MANOVA analyses of the relations between perceptions of parental control and self-reports of "learning in school" showed a significant main effect for perceived parental control of the personal domain. Students who reporting having learned a "little" reported greater degrees of parental involvement over personal domain issues than students who perceived having "learned very much." This trend was also evidenced in a significant negative bivariate correlation of $-.14$ between perceived parental intrusion into personal domain issues and perceived learning in school. There were no significant effects for perceptions of learning in school associated with parental control on the PCDS or ODS. None of the relationships between parental control and academic performance were affected by immigrant status or degree of involvement in Mexican culture.

Parental Control and Self-Reported Grades. The self-reports of perceived learning in school were mirrored in students' self-reported grades. Significant associations between perceived parental control and grades were found for control over the personal domain and overlapping issues. Students who reported receiving mostly grades of D also reported experiencing significantly greater parental control over personal and overlapping issues than did students who received grades of C or better. Again, immigrant children and Mexican Americans with high degrees of cultural involvement reported greater amounts of parental control than Mexican American children who reported less involvement with Mexican culture. However, the within-group patterns were statistically identical with one another. In relative terms within a given cultural frame, the children experiencing the greatest amount of control over personal and overlapping issues also reported receiving poor grades.

The anticipated negative effects of parental undercontrol of prudential and conventional issues could not be confirmed. The one indication that undercontrol was associated with negative impact on academic performance was with students who reported receiving failing grades. Students receiving grades of F reported much less parental control over prudential/conventional and overlapping issues than did other students. However, there were so few students reporting failing grades that this finding could not be verified through inferential statistics.

As Lins-Dyer (2003) had expected, her study with Mexican immigrant and Mexican American children confirmed earlier reports on the deleterious effects of parental overcontrol of adolescents. Her study also demonstrated that the effects of parental overcontrol are not a function of control in general but rather the extension of parental control into the personal areas of adolescents. Moreover, her study offers provocative evidence that the negative effects of overcontrol hold for children and families from traditional, collectivist cultures.

Psychological Symptoms

The final study (Hasebe, Nucci, and Nucci, 2004) discussed here explored the impact of parental overcontrol of personal issues on adolescents' psychological adjustment within the United States and a non-Western culture, Japan. Participants in this study were 170 high school students from a U.S. midwestern suburb and 125 high school students from Akita City, Japan. Akita City is a medium-sized urban center located in a rural surround. The student samples from each country were quite similar in terms of the socioeconomic status backgrounds of their families and the composition of their communities. Thus, the study design reflected an attempt to control for social class in exploring the impact of culture.

The study participants were administered a Japanese or American version of the PAI along with the Brief Symptom Inventory (Derogatis, 1994; Derogatis and Spencer, 1982). This paper-and-pencil measure contains fifty-three items describing psychological problems (for example, nervousness or shakiness inside) and asks participants to indicate (on a five-point scale) how much they were distressed by each problem within the past seven days. Clinicians generally employ this measure as an intake instrument that allows for a quick screening of nine psychological disorders: depression, anxiety, hostility, obsessive-compulsive, interpersonal sensitivity, somatic symptoms, psychoticism, paranoid ideation, and phobia anxiety. The last three scales (psychoticism, paranoid ideation, and phobia anxiety) provide indications of severe psychological disorders that were not included in any of our analyses.

Results from the PAI were concordant with prior work and revealed the following. First, adolescent scores for Idealized Control (Who *should* control the adolescents' behavior?) were lower than their reports of Perceived Control (Who *does* control the adolescents' behavior?) of overlapping and prudential/conventional issues. This is consistent with the general trend for adolescents to wish for more autonomy over such issues than they perceive being granted by their parents. Second, the scores for Idealized Control over personal domain issues did not change with age. Within the high school age group of this study, control over the personal domain is generally viewed as within the adolescents' purview. Scores for prudential/conventional and overlapping issues were lower with age across samples for both the Idealized and Perceived Control indexes. This conformed to the general finding that adolescents claim greater control and experience their parents as providing less control over such issues as children become older. Finally, the patterns were the same across cultures.

Analyses of the relationship between parental control and psychological symptoms revealed the following. In both countries, adolescent judgments of Idealized Control were unrelated to their self-reports of psychological symptoms. There were, however, positive correlations between parental control scores and symptoms for internalizing disorders (depression, anxiety, somatization) and Perceived Control. However, in neither the case of U.S. nor Japanese adolescents was this due to perceived exertion of parental control over prudential or conventional issues. In both cases, negative associations with parental overcontrol occurred with the Personal Domain, and in the case of Japanese participants there was an associated effect with increased parental control over overlapping issues. There were some differences in the expression of symptoms by gender and culture, but the main finding of an association between overcontrol of the personal and internalizing symptoms of psychological problems was similar for adolescents across cultures.

General Discussion

The work reported in this chapter contributes to an emerging pattern of results regarding the appropriate role of parental authority and guidance as a function of the form (domain) of the child's behavior and the child's point of development. What this work (of which the studies reported here are but one part) suggests is that children and parents negotiate a zone of the child's behavior that constitutes a personal domain in which primary decision making is mutually given over to the child. The appearance of a personal domain appears to transcend the particulars of class and culture and runs contrary to stereotypes of cultures as collectivist or individualist (Turiel, 2002). In this developmental respect, at least, all cultures would appear to respect and contain elements of individualism. This is not to argue for a simplistic universalist argument, but rather to acknowledge transcendent aspects of psychology and human development that are part of the objective reality that cultures reflect as much as they affect.

An aspect of that objective reality is that children progressively demand, and parents progressively provide, increased autonomy and self-regulation (Smetana, 2002). Within that process, parents also provide guidance and direction, and on occasion they exert control. Understanding the relationship between what behaviors parents should regulate and what they should give over to the child's discretion adds to the efforts that have recently been made to distinguish between behavioral and psychological forms of control. This work suggests that what psychologists such as Barber (Barber and Harmon, 2002) refer to as behavioral control needs to be circumscribed to those areas of the child's conduct that fall within the moral, prudential, and conventional arenas and that the notion of psychological control needs to be modified to include parental attempts to control behaviors that should be recognized as within the child's personal domain.

The dynamics of development and culture provide a discourse around what behaviors and at what ages an issue should fall within the child's personal domain. The research discussed in this chapter suggests that cultural variation appears to be around the specifics of what is considered to be a matter of prudence or general conventional regulation rather than around the differential treatment of a zone of personal discretion. Moreover, across cultures, there appears to be a general pattern by which the area of the personal is expanded as adolescents mature. To some extent, the variations we witness across groups on these issues appear to be less a matter of culture than of the evaluations that adults make of the perceived prudential risks that their children face. Thus, there is a general trend for lower-class parents to exert more control over prudential issues and for lower-class adolescents to experience greater control over such issues (Nucci, Camino, and Milnitsky-Sapiro, 1996). It is interesting to note in this regard that race may play a role similar to social class within the American setting. Smetana's work with middle-class African American families indicates that African American parents tend to exhibit greater control over their children than do middle-class whites (Smetana, Crean, and Daddis, 2002; Smetana and Daddis, 2002). Nonetheless, even within more cautious or controlling cultural groups, the overextension of parental control to matters that should fall within the child's personal domain appears to have negative consequences for the child.

In sum, the pattern of findings emerging from research on the effects of parental control on children's development points to the efficacy of differentiating between domains of social behavior associated with legitimate social regulation and the zone of privacy and prerogative that comprises the personal domain. The evidence emerging from cross-cultural studies is that establishment of a personal area of privacy and discretion is as critical to healthy child development as is the judicious use of parental guidance and control over the child's behaviors in areas of convention, morality, and personal safety. The interplay, or dialectic, that Baumrind (1971) so accurately captured in her efforts to define parental styles does not take place as a unitary process of negotiation across issues, but rather as a dialogue between parent and child and culture and family among domains of the child's behavior. These domains comprise the conceptual systems the child employs to interpret the social world (Turiel, 1983). These include areas of compromise, collectivism, and moral obligation. They also include a personal zone of individuality essential to the construction of a psychologically sound sense of personhood, autonomy, and individual identity. Sound parenting approaches children's behaviors not in unitary fashion, but rather in a differential manner commensurate with the child's needs for nurturance, guidance, and personal freedom.

References

Barber, B. K., and Harmon, E. "Violating the Self: Parental Psychological Control of Children and Adolescents." In B. K. Barber (ed.), *Intrusive Parenting: How Psychological Control Affects Children and Adolescents.* Washington, D.C.: American Psychological Association, 2002.

Baumrind, D. "Current Patterns of Parental Authority." *Developmental Psychology Monographs,* 1971, 4(1, part 2).

Derogatis, L. R. *BSI: Brief Symptom Inventory: Administration, Scoring, and Procedures Manual*. Minneapolis: National Computer Systems, 1994.

Derogatis, L. R., and Spencer, P. M. *The Brief Symptom Inventory: Administration, Scoring, and Procedures Manual* (Vol. I). Baltimore: Clinical Biomedical Research, 1982.

Dornbusch, S. M., and others. "Single-Parents, Extended Households, and Control of Adolescents." *Child Development*, 1985, *56*(2), 326–341.

Hasebe, Y., Nucci, L., and Nucci, M. S. "Parental Control of the Personal Domain and Adolescent Symptoms of Psychopathology: A Cross-National Study in the U.S. and Japan." *Child Development*, 2004, *75*(3), 815–828.

Kohn, M. L. *Class and Conformity: A Study in Values*. Homewood, Ill.: Dorsey, 1969.

Kohn, M. L., and Schooler, C. *Work and Personality: An Inquiry into the Impact of Social Stratification*. Norwood, N.J.: Ablex, 1983.

Lamborn, S. D., Mounts, N., Steinberg, L., and Dornbusch, S. "Patterns of Competence and Adjustment Among Adolescents from Authoritative, Authoritarian, Indulgent, and Neglectful Families." *Child Development*, 1991, *62*(5), 1049–1065.

Lins-Dyer, T. "Mexican Adolescents' Perceptions of Parental Control and Academic Achievement: A Social Domain Approach." Unpublished doctoral dissertation, University of Illinois at Chicago, 2003.

Lins-Dyer, T., and Nucci, L. "The Impact of Social Class and Social Cognitive Domain on Northeastern Brazilian Mothers' and Daughters' Conceptions of Parental Control." Unpublished manuscript, College of Education, University of Illinois at Chicago, 2004.

Nucci, L. "Conceptions of Personal Issues: A Domain Distinct from Moral or Societal Concepts." *Child Development*, 1981, *52*(1), 114–121.

Nucci, L. "Morality and Personal Sphere of Actions." In E. S. Reed, E. Turiel, and T. Brown (eds.), *Values and Knowledge*. Mahwah, N.J.: Erlbaum, 1996.

Nucci, L., Camino, C., and Milnitsky-Sapiro, C. "Social Class Effects on Northeastern Brazilian Children's Conceptions of Areas of Personal Choice and Social Regulation." *Child Development*, 1996, *67*(3), 1223–1242.

Nucci, L., and Milnitsky-Sapiro, C. "The Impact of Region and Social Class on Brazilian Mothers' Conceptions of Children's Areas of Personal Choice." Unpublished manuscript, University of Illinois at Chicago, 1995.

Nucci, L., and Weber, E. K. "Social Interactions in the Home and the Development of Young Children's Conceptions Within the Personal Domain." *Child Development*, 1995, *66*(5), 1438–1452.

Smetana, J. G. "Adolescents' and Parents' Reasoning About Actual Family Conflict." *Child Development*, 1989, *60*(5), 1052–1067.

Smetana, J. G. "Parenting Styles and Conceptions of Parental Authority During Adolescence." *Child Development*, 1995, *66*(2), 299–316.

Smetana, J. G. "Culture, Autonomy, and Personal Jurisdiction in Adolescent-Parent Relationships." In H. W. Reese and R. Kail (eds.), *Advances in Child Development and Behavior* (Vol. 29). Orlando, Fla.: Academic Press, 2002.

Smetana, J. G., and Asquith, P. "Adolescents' and Parents' Conceptions of Parental Authority and Adolescent Autonomy." *Child Development*, 1994, *65*(4), 1143–1158.

Smetana, J. G., Crean, H. F., and Daddis, C. "Family Processes and Problem Behaviors in Middle-Class African-American Adolescents." *Journal of Research on Adolescence*, 2002, *12*(2), 275–304.

Smetana, J. G., and Daddis, C. "Domain-Specific Antecedents of Psychological Control and Parental Monitoring: The Role of Parenting Beliefs and Practices." *Child Development*, 2002, *73*(2), 563–580.

Smetana, J. G., and Gaines, C. "Adolescent Parent Conflict in Middle-Class African-American Families." *Child Development*, 1999, *70*(6), 1447–1463.

Steinberg, L. "Autonomy, Conflict, and Harmony in the Family Relationship." In S. Feldman and G. Elliott (eds.), *At the Threshold: The Developing Adolescent.* Cambridge, Mass.: Harvard University Press, 1990.

Steinberg, L., Mounts, N. S., Lamborn, S. D., and Dornbusch, S. M. "Authoritative Parenting and Adolescent Adjustment Across Varied Ecological Niches." *Journal of Research on Adolescence,* 1991, *1*(1), 19–36.

Steinberg, L., Mounts, N. S., Lamborn, S. D., and Dornbusch, S. M. "Impact of Parenting Practices on Adolescent Achievement: Authoritative Parenting, School Involvement, and Encouragement to Succeed." *Child Development,* 1992, *63*(5), 1266–1281.

Steinberg, L., and Silverberg, S. "The Vicissitudes of Autonomy in Early Adolescence." *Child Development,* 1990, *57*, 841–851.

Tisak, M., and Tisak, J. "Children's Conceptions of Parental Authority, Friendship, and Sibling Relations." *Merrill-Palmer Quarterly,* 1990, *36*(30), 347–367.

Turiel, E. *The Development of Social Knowledge: Morality and Convention.* Cambridge: Cambridge University Press, 1983.

Turiel, E. "The Development of Morality." In W. Damon (ed.), *Handbook of Child Psychology,* Vol. 3. N. Eisenberg (ed.), *Social, Emotional, and Personality Development* (5th ed.). Orlando, Fla.: Academic Press, 1998.

Turiel, E. *The Culture of Morality: Social Development, Context, and Conflict.* Cambridge: Cambridge University Press, 2002.

Yau, J., and Smetana, J. G. "Conceptions of Moral, Social-Conventional, and Personal Events Among Chinese Preschoolers in Hong Kong." *Child Development,* 2003, *74*(3), 647–659.

LARRY NUCCI *is professor of education and psychology at the University of Illinois at Chicago.*

YUKI HASEBE *is assistant professor in the College of Education at Western Illinois University, Macomb, Illinois.*

MARIA TEREZA LINS-DYER *is assistant professor of psychology at Triton College, River Grove, Illinois.*

3

Adolescents and parents view parents' regulation of some aspects of adolescents' lives as legitimate, but they disagree as to how much personal freedom adolescents should have. Too much parental control over personal issues in early adolescence leads to feelings of psychological control, but increasing autonomy over personal issues in later adolescence leads to better adjustment.

Adolescents' and Parents' Changing Conceptions of Parental Authority

Judith Smetana, Hugh F. Crean, Nicole Campione-Barr

There has been a recent trend in the developmental research on parenting toward greater specificity in defining and assessing parenting constructs. Researchers have called for the need to disaggregate parenting styles and dimensions to examine the component processes that influence adolescent development and adjustment. For instance, they have usefully differentiated between psychological control, or parents' attempts to control the child's activities in ways that undermine his or her psychological development, and behavioral control, or parents' rules, regulations, and restrictions (Barber, 1996, 2002; Steinberg, 1990). Researchers also have examined the different ways that parents obtain knowledge of their adolescents' activities and whereabouts (Crouter and Head, 2002), distinguishing among behavioral control, parental solicitation of information, and child disclosure (Kerr and Stattin, 2000).

Most of this research shares the assumption that parenting styles or dimensions represent relatively stable characteristics of the parent. A number of studies (reviewed by Grusec and Goodnow, 1994, and Smetana, 1997) have demonstrated, however, that North American caregivers (parents and teachers) naturally coordinate their choice of discipline strategy with the nature of the child's behavior or misdeeds and that there is considerable situational variability in parenting. In their influential reconceptualization of parenting styles, Darling and Steinberg (1993) asserted that although parents may use different parenting practices, parenting styles still influence child development and adjustment because they provide an emotional context that changes the meaning of different parenting practices. Nevertheless, the move toward greater specificity in conceptualizing parenting has not included much attention to how parenting beliefs and practices vary as a function of the different acts and misdeeds to which they are directed. Moreover, although the research on parenting has recognized at least implicitly that parents must adapt their parenting beliefs and practices to the increasing maturity and changing needs of the growing child, most research on parenting has not explicitly considered these developmental changes.

In this chapter, we argue for the importance of considering intra-individual and developmental variations in parenting. We focus on adolescents' and parents' beliefs about parental authority and, to a lesser extent, on family decision making, although the distinctions discussed here are relevant to other parenting constructs. The research reviewed draws on the framework of social-cognitive domain theory (Nucci, 2001; Smetana, 1995a, forthcoming; Turiel, 1983, 1998) to outline a domain-specific and developmental framework for examining beliefs about parental authority and their implications for adolescent development and adjustment. We discuss the results of several studies conducted with a sample of African American middle-class families with adolescents who were followed longitudinally for five years. These studies illustrate that different forms of parental authority coexist and follow different developmental trajectories across adolescence and that beliefs about parental authority influence both adolescents' perceptions of parenting and adolescent adjustment.

Conceptual Domains of Parental Authority

Social domain theory (Nucci, 2001; Smetana, 1995a, 2002, forthcoming; Turiel, 1983, 1998) proposes that individuals have different types of social interactions and that their varied interactions lead to the development of different types, or domains, of social knowledge. More specifically, social domain theory has proposed that individuals make distinctions among moral issues, conventional issues, and personal issues. Moral issues are acts that pertain to others' rights or welfare; conventional issues refer to the arbitrary and contextually relative norms (such as etiquette and manners) that structure social interactions; and personal issues, which have consequences only to the actor and are thus viewed as beyond societal regulation and moral concern. Personal issues pertain to privacy, control over the body, and preferences and choices regarding such issues as appearance (clothes and hairstyle), friends, and activities (Nucci, 1996, 2001). Not all issues can be cleanly separated into moral, conventional, and personal, however, and research also has examined how individuals make judgments about issues that entail overlaps among the domains (referred to as multifaceted issues). For instance, keeping the adolescent's room clean, a frequent source of conflict between adolescents and parents (Smetana, 1989), entails overlaps between conventional and prudential issues (for instance, parents may view the room as part of their house and cleanliness as prudentially advisable or tidiness as conventionally necessary), while adolescents may view their room as part of their territory and thus as a personal issue of individuality, identity, expression, or choice. These distinctions, as articulated within the social domain framework, have informed our understanding of adolescents' and parents' beliefs about adult authority. Researchers have examined how adolescents and parents draw boundaries between issues that are seen as legitimately regulated by parents (or other adults) and issues that are viewed as under personal discretion and therefore beyond the boundaries of legitimate parental control.

Much research has shown that morality and social convention are constructed from different social interactions and follow different developmental pathways (for reviews, see Nucci, 2001; Smetana, 1995a; Turiel, 1998). Nevertheless, both adolescents and parents generally agree that parents (or other adults) have the legitimate authority to regulate moral and conventional issues—as long as the authority in question is contextually appropriate (for instance, teachers have the legitimate authority to regulate the child's behavior in school but not at home), and parents do not demand unfair or immoral behavior. In addition, a primary goal of parenting is to protect the child's health and safety (LeVine, 1974). In the social-cognitive domain model, issues of health, safety, and comfort have been referred to as prudential issues. Like moral and conventional issues, adolescents and parents generally affirm parents' legitimate authority to regulate prudential issues (Smetana and Asquith, 1994).

The personal domain is socially constructed through reciprocal parent-child (and parent-adolescent) interactions, including the child's active negotiation with parents. Claims to personal choice originate in toddlerhood (as is evident to parents who have experienced the terrible two's) and continue to develop through childhood. These claims may be particularly important during adolescence, however, because they provide opportunities for the development of individuality, autonomy, and identity (Nucci, 1996, 2001), central developmental tasks of adolescence. Cross-sectional studies conducted in different ethnic groups, including American youth from Mexican, Chinese, Filipino, and European backgrounds (Fuligni, 1998; Smetana, 1988), and in Chilean and Filipino youth (Chapter Four, this volume) have demonstrated that both adolescents and parents treat some issues as under adolescents' personal jurisdiction (Fuligni, 1998; Smetana, 1988; Smetana and Asquith, 1994) and that the boundaries of adolescents' personal domains expand with age. Although parents believe that having personal choice is important for children's developing independence and competence (see Smetana, 2002, for a review), adolescents generally claim more personal jurisdiction than parents are willing to grant.

Developmental Trajectories of Beliefs About Parental Authority

To date, adolescents' and parents' conceptions of parental authority have been studied primarily in cross-sectional designs, leaving open the possibility that age-related differences are due to cohort effects. Recently

Smetana, Crean, and Campione-Barr (2003) examined longitudinal changes in African American adolescents' and parents' beliefs about the legitimacy of parental authority regarding moral, conventional, prudential, multifaceted, and personal issues. Consistent with the increased interest in developmental psychology in modeling development as a continuous process, individual trajectories of change in African American mothers' and adolescents' beliefs about parental authority in these different conceptual domains were examined.

These analyses, as well as others described in this chapter, were drawn from the University of Rochester Youth and Family Project, a multimethod, multi-informant longitudinal study of adolescent-parent relationships and adolescent development in ninety-five middle-class African American families with early adolescents. The families were initially recruited through black churches, black social and professional organizations, and word of mouth in Rochester, New York, and followed longitudinally for five years, with only moderate attrition. Parents and their adolescents were first seen when teens were, on average, 13.1 years of age and again, two years later, when they were, on average, 15.5 years old. They were assessed a third time, three years later (five years after the initial assessment), when adolescents averaged 18.4 years of age.

The families ranged from lower middle class to upper class. Most parents were college educated, and most resided in married, two-parent families, with marital status remaining relatively stable across the five years of the study (for further details on the sample, see Smetana and Gaines, 1999; Smetana, Campione-Barr, and Daddis, 2004). Adolescents and parents judged the legitimacy of parental authority ("Is it OK or not OK for parents to make a rule?") regarding twenty-four hypothetical moral, conventional, prudential, multifaceted, and personal issues, which are listed in Table 3.1.

Latent growth curve modeling approaches were used to examine individual trajectories of change in mothers' and adolescents' judgments of legitimate authority in each domain. (Because there were fewer fathers than mothers in the sample, fathers' responses were not examined in these analyses.) For each of the different types of issues, multilevel models of change were run using structural equation modeling to compare mothers' and adolescents' trajectories of change. The interpretation of results was based on analyses of the intercepts and slopes of these growth curves. We examined differences between mothers and adolescents in both their judgments in early adolescence and in the rate of change over time (accomplished by comparing the fit of the models for mothers and adolescents run with the intercepts and slopes unconstrained and then constrained to be equal). We also examined the effects of mothers' educational background (as a proxy for family socioeconomic status), adolescent gender, and adolescent age at the initial assessment as predictors of change.

We expected that both African American adolescents and mothers would affirm parents' legitimate authority to regulate moral, conventional,

Table 3.1 Stimulus Items Used to Assess Parenting Beliefs and Practices

Moral Items	Conventional Items	Prudential Items	Multifaceted Items	Multifaceted Friendship	Personal Items
Stealing money from parents	Not doing assigned chores	Smoking cigarettes	Not cleaning bedroom	When to start dating	Sleeping late on weekends
Hitting siblings	Talking back to parents	Drinking beer or wine	Getting ears pierced with multiple holes	Staying over at a friend's house	Choosing how to spend allowance money
Lying to parents	Using bad manners	Doing drugs	Staying out late	Seeing friends whom parents don't like	Choosing own clothes or hairstyles
Breaking a promise to parents	Cursing	Having sex	Watching cable TV	Seeing friends rather than going out with family	Choice of music

and prudential issues and that there would be no change over time in these judgments. The results showed the expected patterns. Mothers and adolescents strongly affirmed parents' authority for moral (Ms = .87, .76, respectively), conventional (Ms = .90, .83), and prudential issues (Ms = .88, .78), and for each domain and respondent, judgments did not change significantly over time. Mothers consistently viewed themselves as having more legitimate authority over these issues than did their adolescents.

Mothers of boys and mothers with more education judged parents as having more legitimate authority over moral, conventional, and prudential issues at the initial assessment than did mothers of girls or mothers with less education. Some have claimed that the transition to adolescence and the accompanying physical changes of puberty may carry special risks for African American boys in terms of escalations in racism and prejudice (Boyd-Franklin and Franklin, 1990). Mothers may have been attempting to protect their sons from the external threats of racism, as well as from the higher rates of problem behavior and delinquency found among adolescent boys than girls. The findings for mothers' education are inconsistent with previous research, however, which has shown that higher socioeconomic status is associated with more child-centered and less parent-unilateral parenting (Hoff, Laursen, and Tardif, 2002).

The results of the analysis of personal issues also were consistent with theoretical expectations and the prior cross-sectional research. At the initial assessment, the majority of mothers affirmed parents' authority to regulate personal issues. Although their judgments of their legitimate authority declined significantly over time (Ms = .64. .60, .55 for waves 1, 2, and 3, respectively), the majority of responses still affirmed parents' legitimate authority to regulate personal issues.

Adolescents did not share their mothers' relatively restrictive view of their personal domains. African American early adolescents largely rejected their parents' authority to regulate personal issues, and judgments did not change significantly over time (Ms = .36, .37, .27 for waves 1, 2, and 3, respectively). Moreover, as might be expected, mothers of early adolescents who were older at the initial assessment granted their adolescents more personal jurisdiction than did mothers with younger early adolescents.

Finally, there were significant decreases over time in both mothers' and adolescents' judgments that parents have the legitimate authority to regulate multifaceted issues (for mothers, Ms = .88, .86, .66 at waves 1, 2, and 3; for adolescents, Ms = .66, .62, .44, respectively). Similar findings were obtained for multifaceted friendship issues (Ms = .88, .85, .67 for mothers and .64, .61, .32 for adolescents for waves 1, 2, and 3, respectively). Although mothers and adolescents showed the same trajectories of declines in judgments of parents' legitimate authority over time, mothers initially affirmed parents' authority over these issues more than did adolescents.

Thus, across adolescence, African American adolescents and their mothers strongly affirmed parents' legitimate authority to regulate moral, conventional, and prudential aspects of adolescents' lives, while the adolescents consistently rejected parents' legitimate authority to regulate personal issues. African American mothers changed over time from affirming parental authority to regulate personal issues to becoming more willing (but still somewhat equivocal) in granting their adolescents a sphere of personal freedom. Adolescents and mothers were equivocal about whether parents should have the authority to regulate multifaceted and multifaceted friendship issues, and changes in judgments of parental authority occurred primarily over these issues. These issues are at the intersection of conventional regulation and adolescents' personal jurisdiction, and thus the findings reflect an expansion with age in the boundaries of adolescents' personal freedoms and choices.

Do these findings have any implications for parenting or adolescent development? In the following analyses, we extend these findings to demonstrate that parental authority beliefs influence how adolescents view parenting.

The Personal Domain and Psychological Control

As noted at the outset of this chapter, distinctions have been made between parental behavioral control and psychological control. The assertion is that these are different forms of control rather than two ends of a continuum of control. As conceptualized by Barber and his colleagues (Barber, 1996, 2002; Barber, Olsen, and Shagle, 1994), psychological control, which includes parents' intrusiveness, love withdrawal, and guilt induction, inhibits adolescent development by interfering with the development of a healthy sense of self and identity. This description is strikingly consistent with the conceptualization of the personal domain outlined here (Nucci, 1996; Nucci and Turiel, 2000).

Barber and his colleagues have asserted that children require an adequate degree of psychological autonomy to acquire an understanding that they are effective, competent individuals. Nucci and his colleagues have further specified that the psychological need for autonomy, personal agency, and effectance may be satisfied when individuals define an arena of control over personal issues (Nucci, 1996; Nucci and Turiel, 2000). The assessment of parental psychological control has focused primarily on the style of social interactions that undermine healthy development, but the research and theorizing on the personal domain led Smetana and Daddis (2002) to hypothesize that adolescents would feel more psychologically controlled when they viewed parents as overly restrictive and lacking the legitimate authority to regulate their personal domains.

To test this hypothesis, Smetana and Daddis (2002) examined the influence of domain-differentiated parenting beliefs (referred to as *beliefs about legitimate parental control*) and domain-differentiated parenting practices (referred to as *restrictive parental control*) on African American adolescents' perceptions of psychological control. Parental authority beliefs were assessed by adolescents' (combined) beliefs about legitimate parental authority and judgments of their obligations to obey parents, even when adolescents do not agree with parents' rules. Restrictive parental control was assessed by adolescents' (combined) ratings of whether their family has rules (rated on a five-point scale) and how their family makes decisions about different issues, rated on a five-point scale ranging from whether parents decide each issue without discussing it with the teen or leave it entirely up to the adolescent. Judgments and ratings were obtained in reference to the same set of hypothetical moral, conventional, multifaceted, multifaceted friendship, and personal issues described in Table 3.1. (Prudential issues were not included in these analyses.)

Although morality and social convention differ both conceptually and empirically, both pertain to acts that are proscribed for children and adults and are seen as legitimately regulated by parents. Thus, moral and conventional items were combined to form the socially regulated category. Personal and multifaceted issues were combined to form a broad category of personal issues. Smetana and Daddis (2002) predicted that adolescents' perceptions of maternal psychological control (as assessed using items from the psychological control scale from the Children's Report of Parents' Behavior Inventory; Schaefer, 1965) would be influenced by their perceptions of greater restrictive control, as well as their judgments that parents have less legitimate authority over personal issues. Because psychological control has been described as subjective and in the eye of the beholder (Barber, 1996), the analyses focused on adolescents' reports of parenting.

As predicted, hierarchical regression analyses revealed that adolescents who believed that parents ought to have less legitimate control over personal issues and who rated their parents as higher in restrictive control over personal issues viewed their mothers as more psychologically controlling. These findings were obtained in both concurrent analyses in early adolescence and in two-year longitudinal analyses from early to middle adolescence. Moreover, as predicted, authority beliefs and restrictive parental control over socially regulated acts did not significantly influence adolescents' perceptions of maternal psychological control either concurrently or longitudinally. Therefore, psychological control appears to be domain specific and influenced by adolescents' perceptions of parental overcontrol over the personal domain. Although adolescents' claims to personal jurisdiction reflect a normative developmental process, adolescents who believed that they should have more control over personal issues and also viewed their parents as especially restrictive of their personal freedom viewed their mothers as more psychologically controlling.

In turn, other research has indicated that high levels of psychological control predict adolescents' internalizing problems, such as anxiety, depression, loneliness, and confusion (Barber, 1996; Barber, Olsen, and Shagle, 1994). Moreover, in a study of Japanese and U.S. adolescents, Hasebe, Nucci, and Nucci (2004) have shown that perceived parental overcontrol of the personal domain—but not of the prudential and conventional domains—is associated with greater internalizing symptoms, including more depression and anxiety. Thus, research has shown that unduly restricting adolescents' personal freedom is associated with psychiatric symptoms. But the research on permissive parenting consistently has shown that allowing children too much freedom also is detrimental for adjustment. How much personal freedom is healthy and adaptive for adolescent development? We address this question in the next section.

Family Decision Making and Healthy Behavioral Autonomy

This research on parental authority focuses on adolescents' and parents' beliefs about how much control parents ought to have and its implications for perceptions of parenting, but it does not address how much control parents actually grant their adolescents over different types of issues. Adolescents' participation in family decision making has been examined in several previous studies (Dornbusch, Ritter, Mont-Reynaud, and Chen, 1990; Lamborn, Dornbusch, and Steinberg, 1996).

These studies consistently report that youth-alone decision making is associated with negative outcomes and poorer adjustment for adolescents of different ethnicities. In the prior research, however, the measures of family decision making have not been delineated according to conceptual domains. Smetana, Campione-Barr, and Daddis (2004) examined African American adolescents' and mothers' reports of adolescents' decision-making autonomy over conventional, prudential, multifaceted, and personal issues in relation to adolescent adjustment. They hypothesized that African American adolescents would have more decision-making control over personal issues than over all other issues and over multifaceted issues than prudential and conventional issues. They also hypothesized that how adolescents and mothers draw boundaries over the personal domain—and changes in those boundaries with age—would influence adolescents' adjustment.

Previous research with a European American middle-class sample (Smetana, 1995b) has shown that authoritative parents granted adolescents personal jurisdiction over personal issues, but treated multifaceted issues as legitimately subject to parental authority. In contrast, authoritarian parents viewed multifaceted and personal issues as legitimately controlled by parents, whereas permissive parents treated both multifaceted and personal issues as beyond parents' legitimate authority and up to adolescents to decide. These findings suggested that more parent input into decisions about multifaceted issues, particularly in early adolescence, would lead to better adjustment in late adolescence, whereas more adolescent autonomy over personal issues, particularly in late adolescence, would be associated with better adjustment.

These hypotheses were examined using longitudinal data from the University of Rochester Youth and Family Project. Using procedures developed by Dornbusch, Ritter, Mont-Reynaud, and Chen (1990), adolescents and mothers rated how their families make decisions about the conventional, prudential, personal, and multifaceted issues described in Table 3.1 (moral issues were not included in these analyses). Adolescents and mothers rated family decision making on the same five-point scale used in the analyses of psychological control, except that the scores were reverse-coded so that high scores indicated greater autonomy (leaving decisions entirely up to the adolescent).

As expected, both teens and mothers viewed adolescents as having more decision-making autonomy over personal than all other issues and over multifaceted than prudential or conventional issues. Moreover, adolescents overall report having more autonomy over all decisions than did their mothers, and adolescents' decision-making autonomy increased significantly over time, although the developmental patterns varied by domain.

Although many other studies have found that prudential and conventional issues differ both conceptually and empirically, adolescents and mothers did not differentiate between conventional and prudential issues in their ratings of family decision making, except that late adolescents viewed themselves as having more autonomy over prudential than conventional issues. This is consistent with the finding that high school students, and particularly adolescents who have engaged in more drug use, view drug and alcohol use as under personal jurisdiction, even though they may view such behaviors as foolish or harmful to the self (Nucci, Guerra, and Lee, 1991). Autonomous decision making over multifaceted issues increased significantly from early to late adolescence, but on average, and even in early adolescence, these issues were seen as jointly decided rather than decided by parents, with a greater tilt over time toward adolescent decision making with parental guidance. Adolescents' decision-making autonomy over personal issues was seen as increasing with age (and more so by adolescents than their mothers), but on average, adolescents were rated as making decisions about personal issues in the context of parental input and guidance.

Four measures of adjustment were examined: academic performance (as reported by parents); deviance, as assessed using adolescents' reports of their own and their friends' involvement in problem behavior (Mason, Cauce, Gonzales, and Hiraga, 1996); self-worth (as assessed using Harter's 1982, 1988 scales); and depressed mood (as assessed using the CES-D Scale; Radloff, 1977). For middle-class African American youth, healthy adjustment was associated concurrently with continued parental decision-making control over prudential and conventional issues, at least through middle adolescence. Adolescent-reported decision making over prudential and conventional issues was associated with better self-worth in early adolescence and less deviance in middle adolescence.

Similar relationships were observed for multifaceted issues. Greater parental control over multifaceted issues was associated concurrently with better academic performance, better self-worth, and less deviance in early adolescence, with less deviance in middle adolescence and with less deviance and less depression in late adolescence. (The associations for early and late adolescence were found for adolescents' but not mothers' ratings of decision making, while in middle adolescence, the associations were for mothers' but not adolescents' ratings.) Consistent with the earlier research demonstrating that authoritative parents maintain control over multifaceted issues (Smetana, 1995b), these findings suggest that African American adolescents' psychosocial adjustment is enhanced when parents continue to be involved across adolescence (in the context of joint decision making) in decisions regarding multifaceted issues. In contrast, however, decision-making autonomy over personal issues did not show significant concurrent associations with adjustment in either early or late adolescence, although mother-rated decision-making autonomy over personal issues was associated with greater deviance.

Longitudinal analyses indicated that early adolescents' reports of their decision-making autonomy over personal and multifaceted issues, as well as increases in African American adolescents' decision-making autonomy over these issues from middle to late adolescence, predicted better self-worth and less depression in late adolescence. Moreover, similar findings were obtained for the influence of mothers' ratings of adolescents' autonomy over personal issues on self-worth, except that the significant increases in autonomy were found at earlier ages (from early to middle adolescence).

Overall, these results suggest that less autonomy over personal and multifaceted issues in early adolescence, combined with increasing autonomy in middle to late adolescence, predict better self-worth and less depression for African American youth. These findings highlight the need for a developmental framework that specifies the developmental periods when greater parental control, as well as expansion of the boundaries of the personal domain, may be particularly important for adolescent adjustment. Greater control in early adolescence and increasing autonomy after middle adolescence appear to be adaptive for African American youth. It is notable that longitudinal changes in control over personal and multifaceted issues influenced self-system processes (that is, self-worth and depression) but not academic achievement or deviance. Nucci (1996, 2001) has theorized that control over personal issues is particularly important for the development of a healthy sense of self, identity, and agency. It should be noted, however, that the level of deviance was very low in this African American middle-class sample.

Conclusions and Implications

The research discussed in this chapter suggests that adolescents' and parents' beliefs about parental authority are heterogeneous and vary by conceptual domain. Adolescents both accepted and rejected parental authority; mothers' responses, while less extreme in their rejection of parental authority, did show significant variation by domain. These intra-individual variations reflect attempts to integrate an acceptance of parental and cultural conventions and moral values with the construction of self, identity, and boundaries of personal jurisdiction.

Beliefs about the legitimacy of adult authority shifted over the course of adolescence as the boundaries of adolescents' personal domain increased. The developmental and social changes of adolescence lead to many new arenas where limits must be renegotiated and autonomy sought. With age, American adolescents spend increasingly more time away from parental supervision and in the company of peers, and peer relationships are transformed from cliques to crowds and from predominantly same-sex friendships to dating and romantic relationships. These changes may lead to many new opportunities and risks, many of which may be multifaceted and conceptualized in terms of overlapping conventional, prudential, and personal concerns. Adolescents and their mothers both believed that adolescents should be granted more autonomy over multifaceted issues as they grew older; in our view, multifaceted issues constitute the dynamic region where the development of autonomy proceeds.

Although both adolescents and mothers believed that adolescents should have more personal freedom with age, there also were generational discrepancies in these beliefs. African American middle-class mothers (as well as European American mothers studied in other research; Smetana, 1989; Smetana and Asquith, 1994) drew more restrictive boundaries to their adolescents' personal freedoms than their adolescents desired. These discrepancies have been found to lead to conflict in adolescent-parent relationships (Fuligni, 1998; Smetana, 1989; Smetana and Asquith, 1994; Smetana and Gaines, 1999), and conflict, in turn, provides a context for transforming the boundaries of adolescents' personal domains toward greater autonomy.

How much autonomy parents actually grant may depend on a variety of factors, including parents' (culturally influenced) beliefs about the appropriate timing for granting autonomy, their assessment of their adolescent's abilities and competence to assume more privileges and responsibilities, their parenting styles, and their appraisal of the environmental risks of allowing their teens more freedom. These risks may vary in different social contexts, social classes, and cultures, leading to variations in how broadly adolescents are allowed to exercise personal freedom. For instance, interviews with African American mothers indicated that concerns with safety were a frequent and important criterion in their decisions about whether to grant adolescents independence (Smetana and Chuang, 2001). Faced with an environment where racism and prejudice remain pervasive, African American mothers viewed a number of behaviors, such as wearing certain styles of clothes, driving in certain areas or at certain times of day, or being at the mall in large groups of teenagers, as fraught with risks, although these same behaviors might be relatively innocuous personal choices for youth of other ethnicities in the United States. Chinese adolescents in Hong Kong also reported that parents restricted their choice of activities because of concerns about adolescents' safety in the dense urban environment of Hong Kong (Yau and Smetana, 1996). Thus, while adolescents' claims to personal jurisdiction might spur parents to consider granting adolescents more autonomy, parents' concerns with their children's welfare and safety also place restrictions on how much autonomy can be safely assumed. At the same time, social domain theory has proposed (and research has supported) that while there are cross-cultural variations in the boundaries and content of the personal domain, individuals in all cultures assert claims to personal discretion, as having an arena of personal freedom is related to universal needs for effectance and agency (Nucci, 1996; Nucci and Turiel, 2000).

This discussion highlights the complex challenge of parenting during adolescence and the need to consider parenting in a developmentally sensitive way. Parents must be attuned to the developmental changes of adolescence, because control over certain behaviors, which at an earlier age may be seen as appropriate and responsive, might at a later age be viewed as psychologically intrusive and coercive. Parents must strike a delicate balance between providing sufficient behavioral control to keep their adolescents safe, while not being overly intrusive into adolescents' personal domains. Mason, Cauce, Gonzales, and Hiraga (1996) have referred to this balance as "precision parenting." The research described in this chapter suggests that while early adolescents may perceive greater parental control over multifaceted issues as overcontrol of their personal domains, parental guidance over personal issues while allowing adolescents to have the final say appears to be associated with healthy adjustment, at least through middle adolescence. Allowing adolescents more personal freedom as they move into late adolescence appears to promote healthy adjustment. These conclusions are based on research using a small middle-class sample of African American families. Further research with larger and more diverse samples will be needed to replicate these findings.

Finally, the research described in this chapter is consistent with the recent trends toward disaggregating parenting constructs, but it also extends this research to highlight the importance of considering parenting in a developmental and domain-specific framework. In our view, greater domain specificity will add precision to the assessment of parenting and contribute to our understanding of relationships between parenting and adolescent development and adjustment.

References

Barber, B. K. "Parental Psychological Control: Revisiting a Neglected Construct." *Child Development,* 1996, *67*(6), 3296–3319.

Barber, B. K. (ed.). *Intrusive Parenting: How Psychological Control Affects Children and Adolescents.* Washington, D.C.: American Psychological Association Press, 2002.

Barber, B. K., Olsen, J. E., and Shagle, S. C. "Associations Between Parental Psychological and Behavioral Control and Youth Internalized and Externalized Behaviors." *Child Development,* 1994, *65*(4), 1120–1136.

Boyd-Franklin, N., and Franklin, A. J. *Boys into Men: Raising our African American Teenage Sons.* New York: Dutton, 2000.

Crouter, A. C., and Head, M. R. "Parental Monitoring and Knowledge of Children." In M. Bornstein (ed.), *Handbook of Parenting,* Vol. 3: *Becoming and Being a Parent* (2nd ed.). Mahwah, N.J.: Erlbaum, 2002.

Darling, N., and Steinberg, L. "Parenting Style as Context: An Integrative Model." *Psychological Bulletin,* 1993, *113*(3), 487–496.

Dornbusch, S. M., Ritter, P. L., Mont-Reynaud, R., and Chen, Z. "Family Decision-Making and Academic Performance in a Diverse High School Population." *Journal of Adolescent Research,* 1990, *5*(1), 143–160.

Fuligni, A. J. "Authority, Autonomy, and Parent-Adolescent Conflict and Cohesion: A Study of Adolescents from Mexican, Chinese, Filipino, and European Backgrounds." *Developmental Psychology,* 1998, *34*(4), 782–792.

Grusec, J. E., and Goodnow, J. J. "The Impact of Parental Discipline Methods on the Child's Internalization of Values: A Reconceptualization of Current Points of View." *Developmental Psychology,* 1994, *30*(1), 4–19.

Harter, S. "The Perceived Competence Scale for Children." *Child Development,* 1982, *53*(1), 87–97.

Harter, S. *The Self-Perception Profile Scale for Adolescents.* Denver: University of Denver, 1988.

Hasebe, Y., Nucci, L., and Nucci, M. S. "Parental Control of the Personal Domain and Adolescent Symptoms of Psychopathology." *Child Development,* 2004, *75*(3), 815–828.

Hoff, E., Laursen, B., and Tardif, T. "Socioeconomic Status and Parenting." In M. H. Bornstein (ed.), *Handbook of Parenting,* Vol. 2: *Biology and Ecology of Parenting* (2nd ed.). Mahwah, N.J.: Erlbaum, 2002.

Kerr, M., and Stattin, H. "What Parents Know, How They Know It, and Several Forms of Adolescent Adjustment: Further Support for a Reinterpretation of Monitoring." *Developmental Psychology,* 2000, *36*(3), 366–380.

Lamborn, S. D., Dornbusch, S. M., and Steinberg, L. "Ethnicity and Community Context as Moderators of the Relations Between Family Decision Making and Adolescent Adjustment." *Child Development,* 1996, *67*(2), 283–301.

LeVine, R. "Parental Goals: A Cross-Cultural View." *Teachers College Record,* 1974, *76*(2), 226–239.

Mason, C. A., Cauce, A. N., Gonzales, N., and Hiraga, Y. "Neither Too Sweet Nor Too Sour: Problem Peers, Maternal Control, and Problem Behavior in African American Adolescents." *Child Development,* 1996, *67*(5), 2115–2130.

Nucci, L. P. "Morality and Personal Freedom." In E. S. Reed, E. Turiel, and T. Brown (eds.), *Values and Knowledge.* Mahwah, N.J.: Erlbaum, 1996.

Nucci, L. P. *Education in the Moral Domain.* Cambridge: Cambridge University Press, 2001.

Nucci, L. P., Guerra, N., and Lee, J. "Adolescent Judgments of the Personal, Prudential, and Normative Aspects of Drug Usage." *Developmental Psychology,* 1991, *27*(5), 841–848.

Nucci, L. P., and Turiel, E. "The Moral and the Personal: Sources of Social Conflicts." In L. P. Nucci, G. B. Saxe, and E. Turiel (eds.), *Culture, Thought, and Development.* Mahwah, N.J.: Erlbaum, 2000.

Radloff, L. "The CES-D Scale: A Self-Report Depression Scale for Research in the General Population." *Applied Psychological Measurement,* 1977, *1*(3), 385–401.

Schaefer, E. S. "Children's Reports of Parental Behavior: An Inventory." *Child Development,* 1965, *36*(2), 413–424.

Smetana, J. G. "Adolescents' and Parents' Conceptions of Parental Authority." *Child Development,* 1988, *59*(2), 321–335.

Smetana, J. G. "Adolescents' and Parents' Reasoning About Actual Family Conflict." *Child Development,* 1989, *60*(5), 1052–1067.

Smetana, J. G. "Morality in Context: Abstractions, Ambiguities, and Applications." In R. Vasta (ed.), *Annals of Child Development* (Vol. 10). London: Jessica Kingsley Publishers, 1995a.

Smetana, J. G. "Parenting Styles and Conceptions of Parental Authority During Adolescence." *Child Development,* 1995b, *66*(2), 299–316.

Smetana, J. G. "Parenting and the Development of Social Knowledge Reconceptualized: A Social Domain Analysis." In J. E. Grusec and L. Kuczynski (eds.), *Parenting and the Internalization of Values.* New York: Wiley, 1997.

Smetana, J. G. "Culture, Autonomy, and Personal Jurisdiction in Adolescent-Parent Relationships." In H. W. Reese and R. Kail (eds.), *Advances in Child Development and Behavior* (Vol. 29). Orlando, Fla.: Academic Press, 2002.

Smetana, J. G. "Social-Cognitive Domain Theory: Consistencies and Variations in Children's Moral and Social Judgments." In M. Killen and J. G. Smetana (eds.), *Handbook of Moral Development.* Mahwah, N.J.: Erlbaum, forthcoming.

Smetana, J. G., and Asquith, P. "Adolescents' and Parents' Conceptions of Parental Authority and Adolescent Autonomy." *Child Development,* 1994, *65*(4), 1147–1162.

Smetana, J. G., Campione-Barr, N., and Daddis, C. "Longitudinal Development of Family Decision-Making: Defining Healthy Behavioral Autonomy for Middle Class African American Adolescents." *Child Development,* 2004, *75*(5), 1–17.

Smetana, J. G., and Chuang, S. "Middle-Class African American Parents' Conceptions of Parenting in the Transition to Adolescence." *Journal of Research on Adolescence,* 2001, *11*(2), 177–198.

Smetana, J. G., Crean, H. F., and Campione-Barr, N. "African American Middle Class Families' Changing Conceptions of Parental Authority." Paper presented at the Biennial Meetings of the Society for Research in Child Development, Tampa, Fla., Apr. 2003.

Smetana, J. G., and Daddis, C. "Domain-Specific Antecedents of Psychological Control and Parental Monitoring: The Role of Parenting Beliefs and Practices." *Child Development,* 2002, *73*(2), 563–580.

Smetana, J. G., and Gaines, C. "Adolescent-Parent Conflict in Middle-Class African American Families." *Child Development,* 1999, *70*(6), 1447–1463.

Steinberg, L. "Interdependency in the Family: Autonomy, Conflict, and Harmony in the Parent-Adolescent Relationship." In S. S. Feldman and G. R. Elliot (eds.), *At the Threshold: The Developing Adolescent.* Cambridge, Mass.: Harvard University Press, 1990.

Turiel, E. *The Development of Social Knowledge: Morality and Convention.* Cambridge: Cambridge University Press, 1983.

Turiel, E. "Moral Development." In W. Damon (ed.), *Handbook of Child Psychology,* Vol. 3. N. Eisenberg (ed.), *Social, Emotional, and Personality Development* (5th ed.). New York: Wiley, 1998.

Yau, J., and Smetana, J. G. "Adolescent-Parent Conflict Among Chinese Adolescents in Hong Kong." *Child Development,* 1996, *67*(3), 1262–1275.

JUDITH SMETANA is professor of psychology and pediatrics and director of the developmental psychology program at the University of Rochester, Rochester, New York.

HUGH F. CREAN is at the Children's Institute and assistant professor of nursing at the University of Rochester Medical Center, Rochester, New York.

NICOLE CAMPIONE-BARR is a doctoral candidate in developmental psychology at the University of Rochester, Rochester, New York.

4

*With age, Chilean, Filipino, and U.S. youth come to
believe that fewer issues are legitimately within the
control of parents and that they are less obliged to obey
parental rules. These beliefs vary across domains and
countries, providing insight into parent-adolescent
conflict and the development of autonomy.*

Rules, Legitimacy of Parental Authority, and Obligation to Obey in Chile, the Philippines, and the United States

Nancy Darling, Patricio Cumsille, Liane Peña-Alampay

All cultures have a period when children learn to function autonomously and prepare to take on the roles they will have as adults (Schlegel, 1995). As they move from childhood to adulthood, adolescents demand, and parents grant them, increasing autonomy. The ability to function autonomously is a central task of adolescence, and all theoretical perspectives on adolescent socialization and development emphasize the problems associated with failure to successfully negotiate that passage (Zimmer-Gembeck and Collins, 2003). The construct of autonomy, however, is conceptually complex in that it is both multidimensional and strongly linked to other indicators of psychosocial functioning. For example, autonomy encompasses cognitive, behavioral, and emotional dimensions and includes adolescents' behavioral self-regulation, aspects of identity development, and beliefs about parents as individuals separate from the self (Sessa and Steinberg, 1991). In addition, autonomy develops unevenly across different areas of individuals' lives, even within specific dimensions. For example, an adolescent may be highly autonomous in sexual decision making, but be dependent on her parents in

The work reported in this chapter was funded by Fondo Nacional de Desarrollo Científico y Tecnológico Grants 1010933 and 7010933, Chile; the Johann Jacobs Foundation; and the Pennsylvania State University Family Consortium. Special thanks to Douglas Coatsworth and Erin Haley Sharp for their invaluable help on this project.

other areas, such as finances. Arnett and Taber (1994) have argued that unevenness in the achievement of autonomy across different areas of young peoples' lives may be particularly characteristic of modern industrial societies and may constitute a new developmental stage of semidependency, or emerging adulthood.

Conflict and the Negotiation of Autonomy

Our everyday use of the word *autonomy* reflects its complexity. Researchers use the term *autonomy* to refer to a characteristic of the individual. In everyday language, however, we talk about parents "granting autonomy" to their adolescents—in other words, freeing them from external rules or constraints. Although both parents' and adolescents' expectations for adolescent autonomy increase with age, adolescents typically demand autonomy earlier than their parents are ready to grant it. Conflict between parents and adolescents is one marker of the negotiation between adolescents' and parents' definition of the boundaries of adolescent autonomy (Collins and others, 1997). Research on parents' and adolescents' beliefs about the legitimate domains of parental authority (for example, Nucci, Killen, and Smetana, 1996; Smetana, 1988) suggests that both parents and adolescents agree that parents can (and indeed should) regulate some aspects of their adolescents' lives. Other areas, however, are considered outside the legitimate domain of parental authority. For example, both parents and adolescents agree that parents have the right to control youth with regard to safety issues and issues of morality, concede some parental legitimacy to the control of conventional behavior, but agree that parents do not have the right to regulate areas in the personal domain. However, parents and adolescents disagree about which domain a particular issue falls within. For example, how one dresses for church might be seen as a matter of personal taste for an adolescent but a matter of convention for the adolescent's parent. Smetana, Crean, and Campione-Barr (Chapter Three, this volume) suggest that conflict occurs when parents try to control areas of adolescents' lives that adolescents consider to be outside the legitimate domain of parental authority.

Is parent-adolescent conflict most likely to occur when parents exert authority over areas where youth believe they do not have legitimate authority? Cumsille, Darling, and Peña-Alampay (2002) addressed this question directly in a comparative study of 205 Chilean and 122 Filipino adolescents. Cross-cultural research allows study of the expression of autonomy through conflict in cultures that differ in social norms and family functioning. In a meta-analysis comparing individualism and collectivism cross-culturally, Oyserman, Coon, and Kemmelmeier (2002) concluded that Chileans placed a higher value on individualism than do respondents from the United States, who in turn were more individualistic than respondents from Asia (no specific comparison was available with the Philippines). Collectivism, which was assessed independently and was not conceptualized as at the opposing end of the spectrum of individualism, was reported to be higher in Chile and Asia than in the United States. Both individualistic and collectivistic values are thought to be intimately tied to the development of autonomy, with individuals holding strongly individualistic beliefs expecting to be granted behavioral autonomy earlier than those who do not (Zimmer-Gembeck and Collins, 2003). Cultures also differ in their expectations about the relationship between parents and children. Filipino culture places a strong value on children acting toward parents out of *utang na loob,* a debt of gratitude that cannot be repaid, and with *hiya,* or behaving with propriety to avoid shaming one's family (Medina, 2001). Taken together, these findings suggest that Chilean youth may expect autonomy at an earlier age than Filipinos and be more likely to express disagreement with parents.

Chilean and Filipino adolescents (age range, 11 to 23 years; average age, 15.9) were recruited from public schools, private schools, and universities and completed a series of questionnaires. For each of thirty-eight issues, students reported on whether parents had set clear rules or expectations (assessed in terms of yes or no responses), whether it was okay for parents to set rules about that issue (yes or no responses), whether they were obliged to obey rules that they disagreed with (yes or no responses), and how frequently they had discussed or argued with their parents in the past thirty days (zero to three or more times). Initial analyses confirmed clear cultural differences in both parents' granting of autonomy (setting rules) and adolescents' assumption of it (legitimacy of parental authority, measured by adolescents answering yes to whether it was okay for parents to set rules and that adolescents were obligated to obey). As expected, Filipino parents were more likely to set rules, and Filipino youth were more likely than Chileans to believe it was okay for parents to do so and feel obliged to obey rules ($p \leq .000$). Unexpectedly, however, Filipino youth were also more likely than Chileans to report arguing with their parents ($p \leq .000$).

If Filipino culture strongly fosters obedience to parents and Filipino youth are more likely to grant parents legitimate authority, why are Filipino parents and adolescents more likely to argue? The answer appears to lie at the social intersection of autonomy: parents' rules and adolescents' felt obligation to obey. Adolescents reported higher conflict in two conditions. First, conflict was higher around issues for which parents had set explicit rules. Second, conflict was higher around issues that were not governed by explicit rules, but about which adolescents felt obliged to obey. In other words, conflict occurred in the presence of parental attempts to limit adolescent autonomy. Importantly, the highest level of conflict was reported around issues that adolescents felt their parents did not have legitimate authority over but that adolescents felt obliged to obey. This was true in both Chile and the Philippines. Thus, although the processes underlying parent-adolescent conflict were the same for Chileans and Filipinos, the likelihood that conflict would occur was smaller in Chile than in the

Philippines. Chilean parents were less likely to assert control through rules, and Chilean youth were less likely to feel obliged to obey them when they did, thus averting the need for direct confrontation. Filipino parents were more likely to set rules, and adolescents were more likely to believe they should obey them, resulting in higher levels of conflict. The patterning of results suggests that adolescents choose to argue with parents when they implicitly recognize their authority and hope to negotiate for greater autonomy. This is consistent with other research suggesting that adolescents choose to disclose disagreement to parents, rather than avoiding disclosure or lying, when issues are governed by rules, when they believe parents have legitimate authority over the issues, and when they feel obliged to obey (Darling, Hames, and Cumsille, 2000). Conflict reflects the moving edge in the negotiation of autonomy between parents and adolescents.

The Different Faces of Autonomy: Rules, Legitimacy of Parental Authority, and Obligation to Obey

How does parents' granting of autonomy and adolescents' assertion of autonomy differ across different age groups? How are they related to one another? Does this vary by country? Do these aspects of autonomy differ within individuals? To address these questions, students in three large cities in Chile, the Philippines, and the United States (Santiago, Manila, and Miami, respectively) were recruited through public and private secondary schools and private universities through classroom announcements and letters sent to their homes. Three hundred seventy-two Chilean ages thirteen to twenty years, 153 Filipino ages thirteen to twenty years, and 204 American ages fifteen to twenty years participated in the study. Santiago and Manila are quite ethnically homogeneous, and ethnicity was therefore not measured. Within the United States, 51 percent of the sample self-identified as Hispanic (34 percent Cuban), 28 percent as white, 6 percent as African American, less than 1 percent as Asian American, and 16 percent as other or did not provide information on their ethnicity. Overall, 56 percent of the sample was female.

Students completed a questionnaire in classrooms outside the regular school schedule. As part of this questionnaire, adolescents answered nine questions about each of twenty different issues. Questions examined here included assessments of rules ("Do your parents have clear rules or expectations about this issue?"), legitimacy of parental authority ("Is it OK for [your] parents to set rules?"), and obligation to obey ("If you and your parents disagree do you HAVE TO obey?"). Responses were coded 0 for no and 1 for yes. Issues were selected to represent areas that are frequent sources of parent-adolescent conflict and were identified through review of the extant literature (Smetana, 1993; Smetana and Berent, 1993) and focus groups in each country. The cultural appropriateness of stems and questions was validated in a separate pilot study.

Because it had been hypothesized that youths whose parents are authoritative (warm, strict, but granting psychological autonomy) would also be more likely to believe parental authority was legitimate and they were obliged to obey (Darling and Steinberg, 1993), three dimensions of parenting associated with authoritativeness were assessed using a nine-item measure (examples: "I can count on them to help when me I have a problem," "My parents really expect me to follow family rules," "They believe I have a right to my own point of view"). Responses ranged from 1 (*strongly disagree*) to 5 (*strongly agree*). Adolescents reported separately on mothers and fathers, and the scores were combined.

The Interrelationship of Rules, Legitimacy of Parental Authority, and Obligation to Obey. In order to address questions about the interrelationship of rules, legitimacy of parental authority, and obligation to obey over age and across countries, separate three-level hierarchical linear model (HLM) analyses were performed for each country. In these analyses, the issue was nested within autonomy indicator, which was nested within person. HLM was used to estimate each indicator of autonomy across issues, test for differences between each indicator of autonomy, and predict autonomy from between-person differences in gender, age, and authoritativeness. The percentage of issues adolescents indicated were governed by rules, legitimately governed by parental authority, and that they were obliged to obey were graphed by age and country (Figure 4.1) controlling for authoritativeness and gender. In this graph, lower percentages indicate greater autonomy.

As can be seen in Figure 4.1, the relationship between rules, legitimacy, and obligation to obey differed by age and by country. In Chile, adolescents reported that more issues were governed by rules than they believed were legitimately within the control of parental authority ($p \leq .000$) or they believed they were obliged to obey in case of disagreement ($p \leq .005$). Overall, the differences among the three indicators of autonomy did not vary by age ($p > .32$), although the predicted means converge by age nineteen. In sum, all indicators of autonomy increased with age, parents were less likely to grant autonomy than adolescents were to demand it, but by late adolescence, parents and adolescents seemed to reach a common point.

Like Chilean youths, parents in the Philippines were more likely to set rules than adolescents were to believe that they were obliged to obey them ($p \leq .000$). Rules did not differ by age. Adolescents were more likely to believe that issues were within the legitimate domain of parental authority than they were to believe they were obliged to obey ($p \leq .01$). Rules and legitimacy did not differ from one another ($p = .25$). The difference between the likelihood that parents would set rules and adolescents' beliefs that it was legitimate for parents to do so and that they should obey was larger for older than for younger adolescents ($p \leq .05$). In sum, the difference between parents' attempts to regulate adolescent behavior and adolescents' willingness to comply with parental regulation grows larger over adolescence.

Figure 4.1. Percentage of Issues Adolescents Report Are Governed by Parental Rules, Are Legitimately Subject to Parental Authority, and They Feel Obliged to Obey in Case of Disagreement by Age and Country

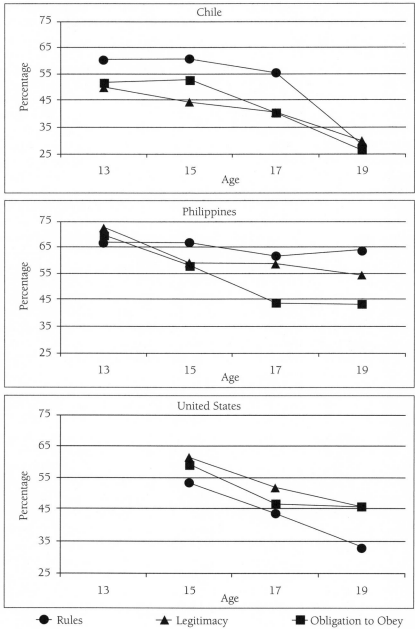

In contrast to Chile and the Philippines, adolescents in the United States were more likely to believe their parents had legitimate authority over an issue than their parents were to set a rule ($p = .001$) or to believe that they were obliged to obey rules they disagreed with ($p = .04$). There was no significant difference between U.S. adolescents' beliefs that they were obliged to obey and the likelihood that their parents set rules ($p = .19$). As in Chile, the relationship between the three indicators of autonomy did not vary by age ($p < .12$). Comparing the three countries, parents in Chile and the Philippines appear to grant adolescents autonomy more slowly than youth believe they should. In the United States, parents grant autonomy at an earlier age than adolescents demand it

Within-Person Differences in Autonomy. A central component of social-cognitive domain is the idea that individuals' beliefs about the legitimacy of parental authority will vary across different domains (Nucci, Killen, and Smetana, 1996; Turiel, 1983). Within social-cognitive domain theory, one's reasoning about an issue, and therefore beliefs about the legitimacy of parents' attempts to exert control over the issue, depend on domain categorization. The focus of prior research in this area has been on normative shifts in adolescents' and parents' reasoning about areas of conflict and beliefs about the legitimacy of parental attempts to control behavior (Smetana, 1988, 1993). For example, the moral domain is governed by principles thought to be obligatory, universally applicable, and impersonal. Doing physical or psychological harm to others is an example of a moral violation. In contrast, the conventional domain is governed by arbitrary or socially constructed agreements about appropriate behavior. Issues within the psychological domain are often conceptualized as outside both moral or conventional control because they affect only the individual. The psychological domain can be differentiated into three subdomains: the personal, prudential, and psychological. The personal domain, which includes behaviors that affect only the self, is exemplified by choice of friends or recreational activities. The prudential domain encompasses issues that have immediate and negative consequences for the self. Some issues are multidimensional, including aspects of both the personal and the conventional. On the basis of this research, it would be expected that parents would grant, and adolescents would expect, greater autonomy in the psychological domain, particularly the personal, than in the conventional domain.

Consistent with earlier research, pilot research in the United States, Chile, and the Philippines revealed that there was little variability in adolescents' reports of conflict or legitimacy in the moral domain (hurting other people or stealing, for example), leading us to drop moral issues from our current study. A series of factor analyses of adolescents' responses to questions about the legitimacy of parental authority done in a sample of 121 U.S. adolescents and of the current data suggested that adolescents' responses to issues could be meaningfully classified into one of five domains: prudential (smoking, alcohol, and drug use), parent expectations (time on the telephone, homework, school performance), personal (choice of friends, dress, use of free time, extracurricular activities, use of money), multiple-domain (type of video viewed, spending time with people parents don't like, unsupervised time with friends, where you go with friends, hanging out after school and after dinner, curfew), and opposite-sex relations ("Your relationships with the opposite sex [phone calls, going to dances or out with mixed-sex groups, dating]" and "Your relationship with your boyfriend or girlfriend [time you spend together, privacy you are allowed, how serious you are, your sexual relationship]").

A series of HLM analyses was calculated in order to predict within-person differences in each indicator of autonomy as a function of domain. In these analyses, responses to personal, parent expectation, opposite-sex, and multiple-domain issues were contrasted with those in the prudential domain. Analyses were performed separately by country. The percentages of issues governed by rules that adolescents believe are legitimately subject to parental authority and that adolescents believe they are obliged to obey in case of disagreement are graphed in Figure 4.2. These percentages control for age, gender, and authoritativeness.

Parents in all three countries were more likely to set rules in the prudential domain than in other domains (Figure 4.2, top panel). Chilean parents were less likely to set rules in the prudential domain than were parents in the Philippines or the United States, but they were also less likely to differentiate across domains. Adolescents also clearly differentiated between the legitimacy of parental authority in different domains (central panel, Figure 4.2). In the Philippines and the United States, adolescents most clearly differentiated between the prudential domain and all others. In contrast, the legitimacy of authority that Chilean youth conferred to parents varied more sharply across issues in the Parent Expectation, Opposite Sex, Multidomain, and Personal domains. Within-person differences across domains were similar to those found in legitimacy of parental authority (bottom panel, Figure 4.2). Youth in the Philippines and the United States clearly differentiated between the prudential and other domains. Chilean youth differentiate more sharply across all domains.

These results have several implications when looked at from the perspective of autonomy. First, parents' granting of and adolescents' beliefs about autonomy are clearly differentiated across domains. This is consistent with arguments by Arnett and others that the transition from adolescence to adulthood is uneven (Arnett and Taber, 1994) and the fundamental tenets of social-cognitive domain theory (Smetana, 2002). The contrast between autonomy with regard to prudential and other issues is striking in all three countries. It is particularly interesting that adolescents are least likely to endorse parents' right to set rules or their own obligation to obey rules over multidimensional issues. This domain encompasses issues that have strong elements of the personal domain (for example, unsupervised time with friends, where you go with friends), but which parents typically

Figure 4.2. Percentage of Issues Governed by Rules, Legitimately Subject to Parental Authority, and Obligatory to Obey by Domain and Country

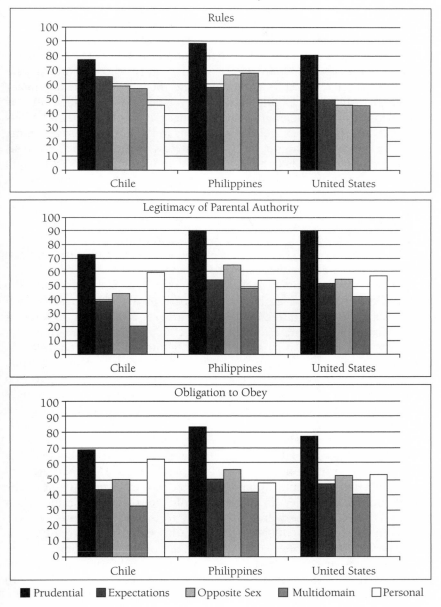

try to regulate for prudential reasons. It is interesting, therefore, that in all three countries and across both legitimacy of parental authority and obligation to obey, adolescents are more likely to exert autonomy in this domain than in any other.

Between-Person Differences in Autonomy. Our focus has been on normative differences in autonomy as a function of age and country. What predicts between-person differences in autonomy? A series of HLM analyses was performed in which country, age, gender, and authoritativeness were used to predict parental rules and adolescents' beliefs about the legitimacy of parental authority and obligation to obey. Age differences have already been discussed. Other demographic differences in autonomy are relatively consistent with cultural expectations. Parents in the Philippines were more likely to set rules than parents in United States, who were more likely to set rules than parents in Chile ($p \le .05$). Chilean youth were less likely to grant parents legitimate authority over issues or to believe they were obliged to obey rules they disagree with than youth in either the United States or the Philippines ($p \le .05$). Gender differences in autonomy were small and were not significantly different across countries. Filipino parents set more rules for girls than for boys ($p \le .05$). In both Chile and the Philippines, girls were more likely than boys to believe that parents had legitimate authority and that they were obliged to obey parents ($p \le .05$).

What of authoritativeness? In prior research, U.S. adolescents who described their parents as authoritative were more autonomous than their peers from nonauthoritative families (Steinberg, Darling, and Fletcher, 1995). However, Darling and Steinberg (1993) hypothesized that adolescents with authoritative parents would be more likely to endorse the legitimacy of parental authority, making them more open to socialization. In this chapter, lower likelihood of endorsing legitimacy of parental authority is seen as an indicator of autonomy. Does authoritativeness predict greater autonomy, controlling for age and gender? In Chile, but not in the Philippines or the United States, parents high in authoritativeness were more likely to set rules ($p \le .001$). In all three countries, adolescents with authoritative parents were more likely to believe that parents have legitimate authority over issues ($p \le .05$). The differences between authoritative and nonauthoritative parents were largest in the United States and smallest in Chile. In Chile, youth who described their parents as authoritative were more likely to feel obliged to obey than those who did not ($p \le .000$). Although authoritativeness did not significantly predict between-person differences in obligation to obey in either the Philippines or the United States, this relationship was not significantly different in those two countries from that in Chile ($p \le .35$). In other words, consistent with Darling and Steinberg's hypothesis (1993), youth from authoritative families were relatively more likely to feel that parents have legitimate authority. There is no evidence that authoritativeness is associated with higher autonomy.

Conclusion and Implications

When examined in the family context of adolescent development, autonomy reflects parents' attempts to regulate their children's behavior and adolescents' beliefs that parents have the right to do so and that they must conform to parental control attempts even when they disagree with them. In three culturally distinct countries, Chile, the Philippines, and the United States, older adolescents are less likely than younger adolescents to believe that parents have legitimate authority over their lives and that they are obliged to obey them in case of disagreement. This is consistent with a growing body of cross-cultural research in this area (for example, Nucci, Camino, and Sapiro, 1996; Yau and Smetana, 2003). It has been hypothesized that this change in adolescents' beliefs about the legitimacy of parental authority, combined with a slower change in parents' beliefs about the legitimate areas of their own authority, contributes to a normative increase in conflict (see Chapter Three, this volume). These results suggest that the picture is somewhat more complex. Conflict appears to be most likely when adolescents do not concede parental authority and (1) parents either attempt to regulate the behavior or (2) adolescents believe they are obliged to conform to parental standards. In other words, if parents do not attempt to regulate behavior or if adolescents believe they do not have to obey if they do, no conflict will occur. For example, although Chilean youth were less likely to concede parental authority, they argued less with parents than Filipinos did, because Filipino parents set more rules and Filipino adolescents felt they needed to obey them.

Autonomy is not a unitary construct in that (1) parents' granting of autonomy and adolescents' beliefs about the legitimacy of parental authority and their own obligation to obey follow different trajectories, and (2) the autonomy parents grant and adolescents assume varies sharply depending upon domain. It should be noted that although most discussions of normative changes in adolescents' beliefs about the legitimacy of parental authority assume that adolescents' desire for autonomy will run ahead of parents' willingness to grant it, adolescents in the United States report that they believe their parents have the right to regulate more areas of their lives than parents try to regulate. It is possible that this reflects the fact that U.S. parents often impose rules only in areas where they seem needed. Thus, parents of youths who are following parents' standards may not need to set rules to gain adolescent compliance to parental standards. In a separate study using the U.S. and Chilean data analyzed here, we examined the predictors of parents' trust (Darling, Cumsille, Peña-Alampay, and Sharp, 2003). In that study, parental trust was assessed as trust that adolescents would use good judgment, not do anything "really dumb," follow rules when parents were not around, act in accordance with parent standards when parents were not around, and tell parents the truth. In other words, it assessed parents' trust that youth would act with responsible autonomy. The number of rules parents set was unrelated to parental trust. However, youths who exercised responsible self-regulation (parent-adolescent agreement, obedience in the case of disagreement, parental knowledge, and low levels of lying) reported higher levels of parental trust. Parental trust may obviate the need for regulation of issues that evoke both the private and the prudential domains. One finding in this chapter that at first seems paradoxical is that adolescents who describe their parents as authoritative are more likely to believe their parents have legitimate authority. If beliefs about the legitimacy of parental authority and obligation to obey are interpreted as indicators of psychological autonomy, these results are inconsistent with previous findings that adolescents from authoritative families are more autonomous than their peers (Steinberg and Silk, 2002). The analyses reported here focus on individual differences in autonomy and control for age, thus predicting the relative autonomy of individuals within age groups. As Steinberg and Silverberg (1987) observed many years ago, early (or premature) autonomy from parents is not necessarily healthy autonomy. It seems sensible that responsible autonomy in adolescents should reflect a clear acknowledgment of the appropriate and protective role of parents. That youth who describe their parents as authoritative are more likely to acknowledge their authority as legitimate is not surprising. Future research should examine the relationship between individual differences in legitimacy beliefs and indicators of psychological autonomy and well-being for youth at different ages and in different cultures.

The development of responsible autonomy is the central task of adolescence from both cultural and individual perspectives. This process is complex, however, and these results suggest that it proceeds unevenly across different domains and depending on what aspect of autonomy is assessed: that granted by parents or that claimed by adolescents. Crossnational comparisons allow insight into these processes and help to increase the variability of our observations so that we do not immediately believe that what is directly before us is all that there is. Although youth in all cultures move toward greater autonomy with age, their paths to that goal vary.

References

Arnett, J. J., and Taber, S. "Adolescence Terminable and Interminable: When Does Adolescence End?" *Journal of Youth and Adolescence*, 1994, *23*(5), 517–537.

Collins, W. A., and others. "Conflict Processes and Transitions in Parent and Peer Relationships: Implications for Autonomy and Regulation." *Journal of Adolescent Research*, 1997, *12*(2), 178–198.

Cumsille, P., Darling, N., and Peña-Alampay, L. "Legitimacy Beliefs and Parent-Adolescent Conflict and Adjustment in Adolescence: A Chilean and Filipino Comparison." Paper presented at the Society for Research on Adolescent Development, New Orleans, La., Apr. 2002.

Darling, N. D., Cumsille, P., Peña-Alampay, L., and Sharp, E. H. "To Feel Trusted: Correlates of Adolescents' Beliefs That They Are Trusted by Parents in Two Cultural Contexts." Paper presented at the Society for Research in Child Development Biennial Meeting, Tampa, Fla., Apr. 2003.

Darling, N., Hames, K., and Cumsille, P. "When Parents and Adolescents Disagree: Disclosure Strategies and Motivations." Paper presented at the Society for Research in Adolescence Biennial Meeting, Chicago, Mar. 2000.

Darling, N., and Steinberg, L. "Parenting Style as Context: An Integrative Model." *Psychological Bulletin*, 1993, *113*(3), 487–496.

Medina, B. T. G. *The Filipino Family* (2nd ed.). Quezon City: University of the Philippines Press, 2001.

Nucci, L. P., Camino, C., and Sapiro, C. M. "Social Class Effects on Northeastern Brazilian Children's Conceptions of Areas of Personal Choice and Social Regulation." *Child Development*, 1996, *67*(3),1223–1242.

Nucci, L. P., Killen, M., and Smetana, J. G. "Autonomy and the Personal: Negotiation and Social Reciprocity in Adult-Child Social Exchanges." In M. Killen (ed.), *Children's Autonomy, Social Competence, and Interactions with Adults and Other Children: Exploring Connections and Consequences*. New Directions for Child Development, no. 73. San Francisco: Jossey-Bass, 1996.

Oyserman, D., Coon, H. M., and Kemmelmeier, M. "Rethinking Individualism and Collectivism: Evaluation of Theoretical Assumptions and Meta-Analyses." *Psychological Bulletin*, 2002, *128*(1), 3–72.

Schlegel, A. "A Cross-Cultural Approach to Adolescence." *Ethos*, 1995, *23*(1), 15–32.

Sessa, F. M., and Steinberg, L. "Family Structure and the Development of Autonomy During Adolescence." *Journal of Early Adolescence*, 1991, 1138–1155.

Smetana, J. G. "Adolescents' and Parents' Conceptions of Parental Authority." *Child Development*, 1988, *59*(2), 321–335.

Smetana, J. G. "Conceptions of Parental Authority in Divorced and Married Mothers and Their Adolescents." *Journal of Research on Adolescence*, 1993, *3*(1), 19–39.

Smetana, J. G. "Culture, Autonomy, and Personal Jurisdiction in Adolescent-Parent Relationships." In R. V. R. Kail and W. Hayne (eds.), *Advances in Child Development and Behavior* (Vol. 29). Orlando, Fla.: Academic Press, 2002.

Smetana, J. G., and Berent, R. "Adolescents' and Mothers' Evaluations of Justifications for Disputes." *Journal of Adolescent Research*, 1993, *8*(3), 252–273.

Steinberg, L., Darling, N., and Fletcher, A. C. "Authoritative Parenting and Adolescent Adjustment: An Ecological Journey." In P. Moen, G. H. Elder, and K. Lüscher (eds.), *Examining Lives in Context: Perspectives on the Ecology of Human Development*. Washington, D.C.: American Psychological Association, 1995.

Steinberg, L., and Silk, J. S. "Parenting Adolescents." In M. H. Bornstein (ed.), *The Handbook of Parenting*. Mahwah, N.J.: Erlbaum, 2002.

Steinberg, L., and Silverberg, S. "The Vicissitudes of Autonomy in Early Adolescence." *Child Development*, 1987, *57*, 841–851.

Turiel, E. *The Development of Social Knowledge: Morality and Convention*. Cambridge: Cambridge University Press, 1983.

Yau, J., and Smetana, J. G. "Adolescent-Parent Conflict in Hong Kong and Shenzhen: A Comparison of Youth in Two Cultural Contexts." *International Journal of Behavioral Development*, 2003, *27*(3), 201–211.

Zimmer-Gembeck, M. J., and Collins, W. A. "Autonomy Development During Adolescence." In G. R. Adams and M. D. Berzonsky (eds.), *Blackwell Handbook of Adolescence*. Malden, Mass.: Blackwell, 2003.

NANCY DARLING is associate professor of psychology at Bard College in Annandale-on-Hudson, New York.

PATRICIO CUMSILLE is professor of psychology at Pontificia Universidad Católica de Chile in Santiago, Chile.

LIANE PEÑA-ALAMPAY is professor of psychology at Ateneo de Manila University in Quezon City, the Philippines.

5

In proposing connections among the paradigms represented by domain theory, parental control theory, and Baumrind's configural approach to parental authority, the worldview of each paradigm must be respected and ambiguities in core concepts must be resolved.

Patterns of Parental Authority and Adolescent Autonomy

Diana Baumrind

Chapters One through Four, all theoretically rich, explore developmental and cultural changes in the boundaries of parental authority that affect development of autonomy during the adolescent transition. In this commentary, I review my rationale for favoring typological analyses of parenting effects based on observational data and suggest how reducing ambiguity in the operational definitions of key constructs in domain and parental control theories could clarify these two influential paradigms further.

A Typological Approach to Parenting Effects

Although I have reported associations between specific parenting practices and child and adolescent outcomes (Baumrind and Black, 1967; Baumrind, 1991), my conceptualization emphasizes person-centered over variable-centered analyses of parenting effects (Baumrind, 1966, 1971, 1991). Accurate characterization of the global form that naturally occurring patterns of parenting practices takes requires sustained observation by judges of family interactions in various settings and social domains, supplemented by probing interviews. Defined by a profile of scores on specific responsive and demanding variables, my configural approach implies a multiplicative, not an additive, relationship among the constituent practices defining each pattern.

Factor analyses of parents' behavior typically yield two orthogonal factors, responsiveness and demandingness (Baumrind, 1996; Maccoby and Martin, 1983). *Responsiveness* refers to the extent to which parents foster individuality and self-assertion by being attuned, supportive, and acquiescent to children's requests; it includes warmth, autonomy support, and reasoned communication. *Demandingness* refers to the claims parents make on children to become integrated into society by behavior regulation, direct confrontation, and maturity demands (behavioral control) and supervision of children's activities (monitoring). Behavioral control and monitoring are modified in their expression and effect on children's development by parental support, reflection-enhancing communication, and psychological control.

Three parenting configurations—authoritative, authoritarian, permissive—emerged from a pilot study (Baumrind, 1967) as empirical descriptions of how parents of children labeled respectively mature, dysphoric or disaffiliated, or immature differed; authoritative parents (of mature children) and authoritarian parents (of dysphoric or disaffiliated children) differed on responsiveness variables, whereas authoritative and permissive parents (of immature children) differed on demandingness variables (Baumrind, 1966). Each of the three parent configurations is a prototype, that is, a complex exemplifying the distinctive features of the group, as well as an explicit description of parenting behaviors that characterize each group member. In a later study (Baumrind, 1971, 1991), a category of disengaged parents who were neither demanding nor responsive was identified.

When the children in my longitudinal study were approximately fifteen years old, I (1991) further differentiated among the four patterns of parents. Based on the degree of imbalance in their demandingness-responsiveness ratio, directive parents were divided into those who were highly imbalanced by being low responsive, high intrusive, and high demanding (Authoritarian-Directive) and those who were only moderately imbalanced, that is high demanding, but moderate-responsive, and moderate or low intrusive (Nonauthoritarian-Directive). Lenient parents were also divided by degree of imbalance with a highly imbalanced lenient type (Permissive) that was low demanding and high responsive, and a moderately imbalanced lenient type (Democratic) that was moderate demanding and high responsive. Two disengaged subtypes, both low demanding and low responsive, were identified: one (Rejecting) hostile and intrusive and the other (Neglecting) indifferent. Good-enough parents were moderately demanding and moderately responsive. Authoritative parents were high demanding, high responsive, and low intrusive.

Adolescents were compared across these eight parent types (Baumrind, 1991). Although youth with authoritative parents were the most competent and least maladjusted, those whose parents were only moderately imbalanced in their demanding-responsive ratio, that is, democratic and nonauthoritarian-directive, were almost as competent and well adjusted. Relative to adolescents from both authoritative and democratic homes, those from directive homes—both authoritarian and nonauthoritarian—were somewhat less individuated and academically proficient but were well socialized. However, children with nonauthoritarian-directive parents were less distressed and more competent than children with authoritarian-directive parents. Thus, consistent with Barber's theory (1996), it was intrusiveness and low parental support, characteristic of authoritarian-directive parents, not high behavioral control characteristic of authoritative and both types of directive parents, that was associated with maladjustment.

Parenting style has proven power to predict children's competence and to qualify effects of (observed) parenting practices other than abuse. Thus, variables representing the demandingness factor were expected to, and did, have a more beneficial effect when embedded in an authoritative configuration than when embedded in an authoritarian configuration; the authoritative, in contrast to the authoritarian, configuration conjoins firm behavioral control and monitoring with warmth and autonomy support. Similarly, high responsiveness affects children positively when conjoined with high demandingness in an authoritative configuration, but not when conjoined with low demandingness in a permissive pattern.

Parenting patterns categorize a particular parent-child relationship at a specific time. However, moderate pattern stability is a likely consequence of continuity in the child's qualities and the parents' values, personality, and expectations. Flexible application of disciplinary practices across domains and infractions varies by pattern, with authoritative and democratic parents likely to be more flexible than authoritarian or disengaged parents in how they regulate a child's behavior.

Parenting Assessed as Action or Conception

Chapters One through Four rely on self-report data. When a single informant provides data on both parents and adolescents, as in the study reported in Chapter Four, the relations between (reports of) parenting behaviors and child outcomes are artifactually inflated.

My typological approach pertains to the sphere of action evaluated by independent observers, whereas the approach of domain theorists pertains to the sphere of judgment from the perspective of family members. In accord with the domain paradigm (Turiel, 1998), both Chapters Two and Three explore how social judgments concerning parents' exercise of parental authority are domain specific in their effects on adolescents' development. Although the major assumptions of domain theory pertain to the development of social knowledge, often in response to hypothetical scenarios, there is an implicit presumption of congruence between social knowledge and social functioning. Thus, Nucci, Hasebe, and Lins-Dyer conclude in Chapter Two that parental authority "is neither perceived by adolescents and children, *nor applied* [italics added] by parents in a uniform fashion across the range of children's behavior."

However, correspondence of judges' ratings of parenting actions and family members' reports of parenting conceptions is likely to be low given the low within-family agreement concerning perceived parenting style reported by Smetana (1995). Therefore, conclusions relating parenting style to family conflict based on parenting measures that assess conceptions of parental authority may differ from those that assess how parental authority is exercised in practice. Two additional studies, which I discuss briefly, illustrate how these differences in approaches can lead to different conclusions. Smetana (1995) assessed conceptions, whereas Sorkhabi (2005) assessed actions.

Smetana (1995) categorized parenting style using a self-report measure to assess predominant style of parental authority as permissive, authoritarian, or authoritative. She then related style to reports of family conflict and adolescent emotional autonomy. Conflict was assessed by asking family members to rate the occurrence and intensity of discussions regarding twenty-four hypothetical transgressions evenly divided among five pure and one mixed domain. Smetana found a main effect of self-reported parenting style on adolescent emotional autonomy and adolescent-parent conflict, with greater autonomy and more frequent conflict predicted by *less* authoritative parenting. Consistent with domain theory, the main effects of parenting style were qualified by a significant domain by parenting style interaction.

In order to determine when and how parenting styles and domains interact in their contribution to parent-adolescent conflict *in practice,* Sorkhabi (forthcoming) examined how parents construct and enforce rules in their own families, as well as the domain of adolescent behavior that parents regulate. She used the adolescent and parent interviews from my study of family socialization to assess (1) kinds of parental rule enforcement (corresponding to authoritarian, authoritative, and permissive patterns), (2) domains regulated (personal, moral, other), and (3) the method parents used to construct rules (unilateral parent, bilateral, unilateral adolescent). Sorkhabi found that parent type explained unique variance in reported conflict frequency over and above both the domains that parents regulated and the method parents used to construct rules. Confirming Smetana's results (1995), all family respondents who described parental rule enforcement as reasoned/authoritative reported the least conflict. Consistent with domain theory, the domains that fathers regulated, according to both fathers and adolescents, explained unique variance in conflict frequency, and only father regulation of the personal domain predicted higher conflict frequency. However, in contrast to Smetana's results, Sorkhabi found no parenting style by domain interaction, and the domains that mothers regulated (according to both mothers and adolescents) did not explain unique variance in conflict frequency over and above parenting styles.

Conceptual and Definitional Ambiguities of Key Constructs

Clarification of the meaning and measurement of the personal domain in domain theory and of psychological control in parental control theory would advance the contribution of each theory to knowledge of how parents influence adolescents' development of autonomy.

Domain Theory. In contrast to the socially regulated and prudential domains whose constituent defining issues are clearly and consensually specified by domain theorists, the issues defining the personal domain are frequently ambiguous, resulting in mixed domains.

In conjunction with Nucci, Hasebe, and Lins-Dyer in Chapter Two, Smetana, Crean, and Campione-Barr in Chapter Three define as "personal" those issues "which have consequences only to the actor and are thus viewed as beyond societal regulation and moral concern." But viewed by whom? Adolescents and parents frequently disagree in practice about what issues should be treated as entirely beyond parental regulation because they have no prudential or socially regulated elements. Domain theorists handle this disagreement by creating a variety of multifaceted, ambiguous, and overlapping domains that include the personal as one element. These mixed domains form a protective belt around the hard core of domain theory because they can be adjusted and readjusted as anomalies arise without threatening its core premises.

A core premise of domain theory is that relative to the regulation of other domain issues, adolescents will view parents' regulation of the personal domain as illegitimate and not obliging obedience, resulting in family conflict and adolescent deviance. However, contrary to prediction, Smetana, Crean, and Campione-Barr found that in response to hypothetical issues, African American mothers affirmed legitimate authority to regulate issues in the personal domain, even with their older adolescents, and also that decision-making autonomy over personal issues was associated with greater rather than lesser adolescent deviance. Also, contrary to domain theory, Darling, Cumsille, and Peña-Alampay in Chapter Four (see Figure 4.1) found that adolescents in Chile and the United States judged a (nonsignificantly) higher rather than lower percentage of personal than of conventional issues to be legitimately subject to parental authority and to oblige obedience. In both countries, the prudential, not the personal, domain differed from the conventional domain in that youths judged legitimacy of parental authority and obligation to obey to be greater in the prudential domain.

When do contradictory results concerning mixed events containing a personal element constitute a challenge to domain theory? For example, Nucci, Hasebe, and Lins-Dyer cite Lins-Dyer's dissertation research findings with Mexican American and immigrant adolescents (2003) to support their hypothesis that the children who report more parental control over mixed (as well as personal) events will receive poorer grades. However, Smetana, Crean, and Campione-Barr, with their middle-class African American sample, found a contrary result in that parental control over mixed (as well as other) issues was associated with better academic performance. Which results confirm and which disconfirm domain theory? Do the contradictory results of these leading domain theorists present a challenge to domain theory, or are they irrelevant to its core premises because they pertain to mixed rather than pure issues?

From my perspective, the proliferation of mixed domains containing a personal element poses an obstacle to definitive tests of hypotheses derived from domain theory. I propose that domain theorists agree on precisely what issues, and no other, constitute the personal domain. Events that contain a prudential, conventional, or moral element from the perspective of a respondent would be classified by that element even if the respondent claimed the event to be beyond parental regulation. With ambiguity caused by mixed events eliminated, hypotheses such as the following could be tested: adolescents, relative to parents, view more prudential and conventional events as beyond parental regulation; authoritarian parents, relative to other parents, view more personal issues as subject to their regulation; relative to persons in individualist cultures, persons in collective cultures view more personal events as subject to parental regulation; and emotionally charged conflict about parents' right to regulate personal issues is greatest in early adolescence.

Psychological Control, Behavioral Control, and Parental Support. According to Barber, Maughan, and Olsen in Chapter One, behavioral control refers to "parental behaviors that are intended to regulate children's behaviors to accord with prevailing family or social norms." Behavioral control is generally associated with greater child competence, whereas psychological control is generally associated with maladjustment. Therefore, the distinction between psychological and behavioral control should be retained. However, the processes instantiating the construct of psychological control are too diverse for optimal conceptual clarity. Constituent processes (see Barber and Harmon, 2002) include, among others, infantilizing the child, possessively restricting the child's activities, guilt induction, love withdrawal, unrealistic expectations, ignoring, and personal attacks. Diversity at a conceptual level is reflected at a measurement level. For example, there is little overlap between Barber's Psychological Control Scale (Barber, 1996) and that used by Galambos, Barker, and Almeida (2003).

Although conceptualized as a measure of parental behavior, psychological control is typically measured (for example, Steinberg and Silk, 2002) as an adolescent perception that parents are intrusive and manipulative. When measured by adolescent self-report, psychological control should be construed as an adolescent variable, not as a parenting practice or style.

Psychological control is not well differentiated from (the converse of) parental support, note Barber, Maughan, and Olsen in Chapter One. Psychological control refers to "parental behaviors that are nonresponsive to the emotional and psychological needs of children and stifle independent expression and autonomy." Parental support, according to Barber (2002, p. 3), includes "nurturance, warmth, responsiveness, acceptance, attachment, and so forth apparently tapping the same central supportive processes that are uniformly related to positive child development." Thus, the two constructs of psychological control and (the converse of) parental support overlap conceptually and in their predicted effects on children's development.

The psychological control processes least likely to overlap with processes defining parental support refer to covert forms of control (typically used by permissive parents), such as emotional manipulation through the use of love withdrawal, guilt induction, and ignoring.

Smetana, Crean, and Campione-Bass remark that the concept of psychological control is "strikingly consistent with the conceptualization of the personal domain." However, the operations that define the personal domain and psychological control differ substantially, even when both rely on the same, that is, self-report, methodology. Thus none of the issues defining Smetana, Crean, and Campione-Bass's or Nucci, Hasebe, and Lins-Dyer's personal domain scales, or classified by Darling, Cumsille, and Peña-Alampay as personal, coincide with those in Barber, Maughan, and Olsen's psychological control scale. However, both superfluous regulation of the personal domain and the hypercritical and intrusive processes included in Barber's Psychological Control Scale are alike in that they are markers of an authoritarian style of control, typically associated with poor adjustment.

Authoritative Parenting and Adolescent Autonomy. The salutary effect of authoritative parents on adolescent autonomy and other attributes is likely due to their unique configuration of high warmth, autonomy support and behavioral control, and minimal use of psychological control. Autonomy support and psychological control are not binary opposites of a single continuum. Not all parents who eschew the use of psychological control are actively autonomy supportive. Neither nonauthoritarian-directive nor authoritative parents are psychologically controlling, but authoritative parents, unlike nonauthoritarian-directive parents, are also autonomy supportive. Authoritative parents are both power assertive in that they enforce their directives and autonomy supportive in that they encourage critical reflection and reasoning (Baumrind, 1991; Darling and Steinberg, 1993).

Previous findings (for example, Baumrind, 1991; Steinberg and Silk, 2002) report a positive relation between authoritative parenting and adolescent autonomy. However, Darling, Cumsille, and Peña-Alampay found a negative relation between authoritative parenting and adolescent autonomy, that is, because adolescents' "beliefs about the legitimacy of parental authority and obligation to obey are interpreted as indicators of psychological autonomy." Adolescents who view parental authority as legitimate, and thus are operationally defined by Darling, Cumsille, and Peña-Alampay as lacking autonomy, also rate their parents high on the authoritativeness dimension. However, when construed as a positive attribute (rather than as the binary opposite of heteronomy), autonomy includes a sense of self-efficacy, agency, and individuation that enable persons to be self-determining. Darling, Cumsille, and Peña-Alampay's unusual results follow from their unusual operationalizations of autonomy and authoritative parenting, so that their results do not imply that parents observed to be authoritative deter adolescent autonomy.

In contrast to a configural (person-centered) measure, Darling, Cumsille, and Peña-Alampay employ a dimensional (variable-centered) measure of authoritativeness, so that respondents need not rate their parents as acceptant *and* autonomy-supportive *and* power-assertive to be described as highly authoritative. Thus, Darling, Cumsille, and Peña-Alampay's self-report measure does not capture the meaning of the authoritative configuration, which contains extra information above that conveyed by a high score summed across the three component dimensions. We do not know how parents classified by parenting type, as Smetana did using the Buri (1991) self-report, would score on a dimensional measure of authoritativeness, or whether being less authoritative implies that parents are more permissive *or* more authoritarian *or* more disengaged.

Conclusion

This conceptually rich volume offers bridging connections between influential paradigms. A research paradigm represents an internally consistent worldview that determines its unique focus of attention, basic premises, and preferred methodology. A core assumption of domain theory is that social judgments draw from multiple domains applied differently in different domains. Control theory emphasizes the critical but often overlooked distinction between psychological control and behavioral control. My paradigm emphasizes the modifying effects of global patterns of parental authority on how specific socialization practices affect children's development.

In this volume and elsewhere, Nucci (1996) and Smetana (1995) have concluded that their findings "lend additional support to the proposal that parenting behaviors are guided by a multifaceted set of concerns for children's social development rather than by an overarching parenting style" (Nucci and Smetana, 1996, p. 1882). Proposing bridging connections among such distinct paradigms risks distorting or subsuming the unique features of one to another. However, information obtained under one paradigm can be used to enrich knowledge derived from another. Thus, Smetana (1995) reported that authoritative parents distinguished most clearly between issues over which they should and should not exert control, tending to be permissive only with respect to pure personal domain issues. Sorkhabi's study (forthcoming) successfully integrated concepts from domain theory and my configural approach to socialization research. Resolution of ambiguities in the meaning and measurement of the core concepts of domain theory and control theory will further enrich the contribution of each to an understanding of the effects of parental authority throughout the adolescent transition.

References

Barber, B. K. "Parental Psychological Control: Revisiting a Neglected Construct." *Child Development*, 1996, 67(6), 3296–3319.

Barber, B. K. "Reintroducing Parental Psychological Control." In B. K. Barber (ed.), *Intrusive Parenting: How Psychological Control Affects Children and Adolescents.* Washington, D.C.: American Psychological Association, 2002.

Barber, B. K., and Harmon, E. L. "Violating the Self: Parental Psychological Control of Children and Adolescents." In B. K. Barber (ed.), *Intrusive Parenting: How Psychological Control Affects Children and Adolescents.* Washington, D.C.: American Psychological Association, 2002.

Baumrind, D. "Effects of Authoritative Parental Control on Child Behavior." *Child Development,* 1966, *37*(4), 887–907.

Baumrind, D. "Child Care Practices Anteceding Three Patterns of Preschool Behavior." *Genetic Psychology Monographs,* 1967, *75*(1), 43–88.

Baumrind, D. "Current Patterns of Parental Authority." *Developmental Psychology Monograph,* 1971, *4*(1, Pt. 2), 1–103.

Baumrind, D. "The Influence of Parenting Style on Adolescent Competence and Substance Abuse." *Journal of Early Adolescence,* 1991, *11*(1), 56–95.

Baumrind, D. "The Discipline Controversy Revisited." *Family Relations,* 1996, *4*(4), 405–414.

Baumrind, D., and Black, A. E. "Socialization Practices Associated with Dimensions of Competence in Preschool Boys and Girls." *Child Development,* 1967, *38*(2), 291–327.

Buri, J. "Parental Authority Questionnaire." *Journal of Personality Assessment,* 1991, *57*(1), 110–119.

Darling, N., and Steinberg, L. "Parenting Style as Context: An Integrative Model." *Psychological Bulletin,* 1993, *113*(3), 487–496.

Galambos, N. L., Barker, E. T., and Almeida, D. M. "Parents *Do* Matter: Trajectories of Change in Externalizing and Internalizing Problems in Early Adolescence." *Child Development,* 2003, *74*(2), 578–594.

Lins-Dyer, T. "Mexican Adolescents' Perceptions of Parental Control and Academic Achievement: A Social Domain Approach." Unpublished doctoral dissertation, University of Illinois at Chicago, 2003.

Maccoby, E. E., and Martin, J. A. "Socialization in the Context of the Family: Parent-Child Interaction." In E. M. Hetherington (ed.) and P. H. Mussen (series ed.), *Handbook of Child Psychology.* Vol. 4: *Socialization, Personality, and Social Development.* New York: Wiley, 1983.

Nucci, L. P. "Morality and the Personal Sphere of Actions." In E. S. Reed, E. Turiel, and T. Brown (eds.), *Values and Knowledge.* Mahwah, N.J.: Erlbaum, 1996.

Nucci, L. P., and Smetana, J. G. "Mothers' Concepts of Young Children's Areas of Personal Freedom." *Child Development,* 1996, *67*(4), 1870–1886.

Smetana, J. G. "Parenting Styles and Conceptions of Parental Authority." *Child Development,* 1995, *66*(2), 299–316.

Sorkhabi, N. *The roots of parent-adolescent conflict: Domain of interactions versus form and patterns of parental authority.* Paper presented at the meeting of the Society for Research in Child Development, Atlanta, Ga., Apr. 2005.

Steinberg, L., and Silk, J. S. "Parenting Adolescents." In M. H. Bornstein (ed.), *The Handbook of Parenting,* Vol. 1: *Children and Parenting.* Mahwah, N.J.: Erlbaum, 2002.

Turiel, E. "The Development of Morality." In W. Damon (ed.), *Handbook of Child Psychology,* Vol. 3: N. Eisenberg (ed.), *Social, Emotional and Personality Development* (5th ed.). Orlando, Fla.: Academic Press, 1998.

DIANA BAUMRIND is a research scientist at the Institute of Human Development at the University of California, Berkeley.

6

The construct of psychological control, important in research on parenting and adolescent development, is much in need of clarification.

Psychological Control: Style or Substance?

Laurence Steinberg

In a series of publications during the late 1980s and early 1990s, I attempted to reorient researchers interested in parenting and adolescent development to the difference between psychological control and behavioral control in both their nature and their consequences for the adolescent (Steinberg, 1990; Steinberg, Elmen, and Mounts, 1989). The distinction—between attempts by the parent to control the child's psychological state and attempts by the parent to regulate the child's behavior—was introduced into the empirical study of socialization by Schaefer (1965) forty years ago. It had become lost over the years, perhaps because widely cited summaries of the socialization literature during the 1970s and 1980s portrayed parenting practices as falling along just two orthogonal dimensions: warmth and control or, as they came to be known, responsiveness and demandingness (Maccoby and Martin, 1983). Responsiveness was often operationalized using measures of parental warmth and acceptance, while demandingness came to be defined with respect to parental firmness. An important component of parenting, the use of psychological control, more or less disappeared from the empirical literature on socialization. Here, I focus on the relationship between parental authority and the adolescent's experience of psychological control, and especially on the ways in which psychological control is defined and measured. In particular, I ask whether psychological control is a matter of style or substance.

Let me begin with the observation, borne out by the other chapters in this volume, that the distinction between psychological and behavioral control is one worth keeping and that measuring psychological control as distinct from behavioral control in studies of adolescent socialization is worthwhile, because variations in behavioral versus psychological control appear to have different consequences for the child (Gray and Steinberg, 1999). More specifically, whereas variations in parents' use of behavioral control tend to be most strongly related to problems in conduct (such as delinquency and drug and alcohol use), variations in parents' use of psychological control are most strongly related to problems of internalization (for example, depressive and anxious symptomatology). Importantly, because healthy adolescent development is associated with higher levels of behavioral control but lower levels of psychological control (Steinberg, 1990), research that employs measures of control that blur the two constructs may yield findings that are difficult to interpret.

The growing recognition over the past fifteen years of the need to incorporate measures of psychological control into assessments of parenting practices has not, unfortunately, been matched by an increase in the conceptual clarity of the construct, as is revealed when Chapters One through Four in this volume are considered together. Independently, these chapters are each quite interesting and internally coherent. But a close reading of them suggests four different conceptualizations and definitions of what psychological control is and how best to measure it. The main point of disagreement centers on whether psychological control is defined by the issues over which parents assert their authority (that is, the substance), a stance favored by both Nucci, Hasebe, and Dyer (Chapter Two, this volume) and by Smetana, Crean, and Campione-Barr (Chapter Three, this volume) or by the manner in which parents parent (that is, the style), a position endorsed by both Barber, Maughan, and Olsen (Chapter One, this volume) and Darling, Cumsille, and Peña-Alapay (Chapter Four, this volume).

The approach taken by Nucci, Hasebe, and Dyer and by Smetana, Creane, and Campione-Barr is, in my view, a substantial departure from historical practice, and it is worth examining in some detail. Traditionally, psychological control has been defined as the assertion of parental authority through the use of emotionally manipulative techniques, such as love withdrawal or guilt induction. Within the social domain approach favored in Chapters Two and Three, however, psychological control is defined by the domains over which parents attempt to impose their authority and not by *how* their authority is asserted. According to this view, when parents attempt to exert authority over matters that the adolescent perceives as personal (rather than conventional, prudential, or moral), the adolescent experiences the parental control as impinging on his or her sense of autonomy and identity, and this, in turn, has deleterious consequences for the adolescent's psychological well-being.

I believe that it is no coincidence that the domain of issues relevant to the adolescent's experience of psychological control is also the domain of issues relevant to parent-adolescent conflict. Although neither Chapter Two nor Three invokes the work of the neoanalytical theorist Peter Blos (1967), that author's writings on the topic of individuation potentially inform our understanding of the process by which parental control over what adolescents perceive as "their business" leads to adverse psychological outcomes for the child. Arguments over personal matters, which comprise the bulk of parent-adolescent conflict, are from this neoanalytical vantage point much more than what they appear to be. In my view, the disputes are not simply arguments over personal matters but, rather, a crucial component of the individuation process. As a consequence, conflict over what otherwise are fairly mundane matters is often imbued with an emotional intensity that is well out of proportion with the significance of the issue. From this perspective, one might hypothesize that adolescents use personal matters as a way of establishing emotional autonomy from their parents, and parental responses to these attempts at individuation affect how successful and stormy the individuation process is likely to be. Perhaps the reason adolescents feel psychologically controlled when their parents assert their authority over personal matters is that these intrusions disrupt the individuation process.

The fact that the personal domain is the focus of most disputes between parents and teenagers allows adolescents to establish emotional autonomy through arguments with their parents about things that are unlikely to become relationship breakers. Arguments over prudential (such as whether the adolescent can drop out of school) or moral (whether the adolescent can have sex with a romantic partner in the parents' home) matters would be much more likely to escalate into unhealthy and perhaps enduring disputes than would conflict over what Hill (1988) referred to as "garbage and galoshes," which is probably pretty short-lived (albeit frequent). In healthy families, adolescents and parents find issues about which they can safely squabble, so that the bickering will foster just enough emotional distance to permit the adolescent to individuate, but not so much that the affective quality of the relationship is threatened. Ironically, then, the developmentally crucial process of adolescent individuation unfolds primarily within the territory of the trivial. This helps to explain the otherwise perplexing (albeit much replicated) finding that it is often the least consequential matters that adolescent and parents have the most emotionally charged fights about.

One fascinating but largely unstudied question is how adolescents' and parents' judgments about which matters are personal and which are not change with development and over time. In this respect, social domain theory may provide a new way of thinking about the vicissitudes of parent-child conflict during the preadolescent and adolescent years. We know, for example, that parent-child conflict increases in intensity between preadolescence and middle adolescence and declines in frequency between early and middle adolescence, making early adolescence the period when conflict frequency and intensity are both relatively high (Collins and Laursen, 2004). One possibility is that this pattern of change somehow reflects changes in the ways in which adolescents and parents define issues as either personal or nonpersonal matters. Prior to preadolescence, children are willing to accept their parents' definitions of borderline issues (those that are not obviously personal or nonpersonal) as nonpersonal. But as Chapters Two and Three show, as children mature, they come to see more and more issues as matters of personal choice over which parents do not have legitimate authority. And, in fact, by the time a child has reached late adolescence, most borderline issues are agreed on by parents and teenagers as personal ones. (For instance, if my college-aged son wants to smoke cigarettes or drink, there is nothing much that I can do about it, and I have no choice but to let this be a personal decision of his. But I would not have looked at this issue this way a few years ago.)

Thus, during the adolescent decade, there is some process of issue redefinition taking place in the minds of teenagers and parents. However, the rate at which this redefinition occurs varies between children and their parents. Specifically, parents' willingness to redefine issues that they see as prudential, conventional, or moral into personal ones lags behind children's desire for this to happen. My hypothesis is that the period of greatest discrepancy is early adolescence, when the rate and intensity of parent-child conflict is relatively high. As parents increasingly come around to accepting their adolescent's view of things, conflict begins to moderate.

If this is indeed the case and if the imposition of parental authority over personal matters is experienced by the adolescent as psychological control, children's reports of psychological control should therefore decline over the adolescent years. But this is not what Barber and others find; his results indicate that reports of psychological control remain stable over the course of adolescence. So the question remains: If parents are relinquishing control over more and more matters that fall into what adolescents see as the personal domain, and if this should make adolescents feel less controlled, why do adolescents' subjective feelings of psychological control, at least as assessed by Barber, not decline over time?

I suspect that the reason has more to do with the different ways in which psychological control is conceptualized and operationalized than with anything else. In contrast to social domain theory, which defines psychological control with respect to the issue over which parents attempt to exercise their authority, the model of parenting practices reflected in Chapter One and, to a lesser extent, Chapter Four, defines psychological control with respect to the manner in which parents exercise their authority. In Barber, Maughan, and Olsen's words, "Parental psychological control refers to parental behaviors that are nonresponsive to the emotional and psychological needs of children and stifle independent expression and autonomy." From this perspective, psychological control is more about style than substance.

In my own program of research, my collaborators and I take a similar stance. We assess psychological control by having adolescents agree or disagree with statements such as, "Whenever I argue with my parents, they say things like, 'You'll know better when you grow up,'" or "My parents act cold and unfriendly if I do something they don't like" (Steinberg, Lamborn, Dornbusch, and Darling, 1992). We do not distinguish between the use of these tactics in personal versus conventional, prudential, or moral debates. Thus, within our definitional framework, a parent could conceivably assert authority over an issue that fell into the personal domain if he or she did so in a way that was noncoercive, and doing so would not constitute the exercise of psychological control. For example, a parent might say to an adolescent in a kind and respectful way, "Please change your shirt before we go to your grandmother's house for dinner." Although the request refers to a domain that is personal (choice of clothing), it does not necessarily expose the adolescent to coercion or emotional manipulation. Whether such a request would be experienced as psychological control, as suggested by social domain theory, or not, as suggested by Barber or myself, is an open question. By the same token, it seems entirely possible for parents to assert control over a prudential or moral issue in a way that is emotionally manipulative and consequently experienced by the adolescent as psychologically controlling. When my mother discovered that I (at the time, a teenager) had been experimenting with marijuana throughout my high school years, she covered her face with her hands and wailed, "I can't believe that you came from my womb." If that is not psychological control, I do not know what is.

Even among those who view psychological control as more a matter of style than substance, there is disagreement about how it should be best conceptualized. It is not clear, for example, that psychological autonomy granting, as operationalized in the research described by Darling, Cumsille, and Peña-Alapay, is the opposite of psychological control as operationalized in the research described by Barber, Maughan, and Olsen. Indeed, in our own work on this topic (Silk, Morris, Kanaya, and Steinberg, 2003), we find that scales measuring psychological control and psychological autonomy granting are only weakly (negatively) correlated and are differentially related to adolescent outcomes. High levels of psychological control on the part of parents, as expected, are predictive of internalizing problems in adolescents, but psychological autonomy granting, surprisingly, is unrelated to adolescent internalization. Low levels of psychological control and high levels of psychological autonomy were independently related to adolescents' positive self-conceptions. These findings suggest that adolescents' mental health and psychosocial development may be adversely affected by high levels of psychological control, but that the encouragement of autonomy by parents may be related only to the development of psychosocial competence, and not to symptomatology. Another way of stating this is that the presence of psychological control is a risk factor for psychological problems, but the absence of psychological autonomy granting is not. I believe this is consistent with the more general principle that it is the presence of negative parenting, rather than the absence of positive parenting, that is predictive of psychopathology in children and adolescents.

Although they approach psychological control from different perspectives, Chapters One through Four clearly lead to the conclusion that psychological control is ultimately defined by the subjective experience of the adolescent. Although all four studies help us understand what it is that parents do that makes their teenagers feel psychologically controlled, in the end, it is how the adolescent experiences these behaviors that matters. My initial expectation was that perhaps the social domain perspective could introduce a bit of objectivity into the measurement of psychological control, but after mulling things over, I ended up concluding that this is not where this perspective is helpful. Thus, although Nucci, Hasebe, and Lins-Dyer define psychological control with respect to parental attempts to assert authority over matters the adolescent views as personal, and behavioral control as attempts to assert authority over matters the adolescent views as prudential, conventional, or moral, it is ultimately the adolescent's opinion as to what is personal and what is not that is important. Indeed, when they write that "the notion of psychological control needs to be modified to include parental attempts to control behaviors that *should* be recognized as within the child's personal domain" (italics added), I can only conclude that the word *should* refers to the adolescent's perception of things. If not, I am puzzled by how, as a researcher, one decides which issues "should" be recognized as personal and which should not, since this will vary as a function of the adolescent's age and the social context in which he or she lives. Smetana, Crean, and Campione-Barr, too, ultimately place the adolescent in charge of defining when he or she is being psychologically controlled, writing that "psychological control appears to be domain specific and influenced by *adolescents' perceptions of parental overcontrol* over the personal domain" (italics added). These authors imply that some degree of parental control over the personal domain is acceptable. But when does control become overcontrol?

In the end, I believe it is prudent to maintain the definition of psychological control as part of the style, rather than substance, of parenting (for more on the distinction between style and substance, see Darling and Steinberg, 1993). Where social domain theory falls short as a perspective on psychological control, in my view, is that it does not really tell us how adolescents (or their parents) decide which matters are worth fighting about and which are not. That is, whereas the theory offers an informative perspective on *what* makes adolescents feel psychologically controlled (parental intrusion into the domain of the personal) and helps explain *why* they do (the intrusion interferes with the process of individuation), it cannot really predict *when* they will feel this way (since adolescents differ with respect to what they consider personal and, presumably, in how they define "overcontrol"). Social domain theory is helpful in pointing out that individuals make distinctions between personal matters and matters that fall into other domains, and it is helpful in illuminating why the nature and consequences of parent-adolescent disagreements vary as a function of the domain in question, but it is less helpful in explaining why individuals, both within and between families, vary in their opinions about what is personal and what is not, or where one draws the line between acceptable levels of parental control and parental intrusiveness. At the extremes, of course, the distinctions are obvious; whether one wears one's hair short or long is clearly a personal matter, but whether one wears a seat belt while driving is obviously a prudential one. But it is not clear how distinctions in less obvious cases are made.

One possibility is that individuals look to one or more reference groups for guidance on these matters. This is implied in the cross-cultural and cross-ethnic comparisons of adolescents' perceptions of the legitimacy of parental authority contained in this volume, but it would be interesting to look at individual differences as well. If, for example, an adolescent discovers that her friends all have different curfews or different understandings with their parents about the acceptability of navel piercing, or different agreements about the amount of time they can spend on the telephone, it stands to reason that the issue must be a personal one (or how else to explain the variability?). But if an adolescent learns that none of her friends is permitted to smoke or that all are expected to attend church services, it would make the issue seem to be less a matter of personal choice. One area ripe for research therefore is the extent to which domain distinctions are similar across families of adolescents who are friends.

I noted earlier that over the course of adolescence, transformations take place in the ways in which both teenagers and parents define issues but that the pace of redefinition varies between adolescents and their parents. A second direction that new work on this topic might take is to examine the impact of this transformation in how issues are defined on *parents'* mental health. In earlier work with Susan Silverberg Koerner (Silverberg and Steinberg, 1987, 1990), we found that struggles over autonomy-related issues were significant contributors to reports of psychological symptomatology and dissatisfaction, particularly among mothers. Whether the relinquishment of authority over issues that had once been in the parental bailiwick is experienced as an unwanted loss of power or as a welcome surrender of authority is an important but unanswered question (but see Steinberg and Steinberg, 1994). Presumably, after years of battling over the state of the adolescent's room, some parents would rather close the adolescent's bedroom door and look the other way than to continue the struggle.

The distinction between psychological control as a matter of style and psychological control as a matter of substance is not a trivial one and merits further systematic inquiry. Both operationalizations of psychological control predict similar negative outcomes for adolescents, but it is not clear if the correlation between these operationalizations is real or spurious and, if real, what the connection is all about. On the face of it, there is no obvious reason to presume that parents who assert their authority over matters that adolescents' generally perceive as personal would necessarily be more likely than other parents also to employ guilt induction, love withdrawal, or other emotionally coercive techniques, or that parents who limit their assertion of authority to the nonpersonal domains also happen to be less emotionally manipulative. My suspicion is that adolescents who describe their parents as asserting excessive control over personal matters also characterize them as psychologically controlling, and that the correlation between the two measures is due to the fact that they both load on a global factor reflecting a negative view of one's parents. Until we have evidence that *parents'* reports of asserting authority over their adolescent's personal matters are correlated with *adolescents'* reports of psychological control (and there is no evidence one way or the other in the chapters in this volume), we cannot tell if the putative link between the two is genuine or artifactual.

References

Blos, P. "The Second Individuation Process of Adolescence." In R. S. Eissler and others (eds.), *Psychoanalytic Study of the Child.* Guilford, Conn.: International Universities Press, 1967.

Collins, W. A., and Laursen, B. "Parent-Adolescent Relationships and Influences." In R. Lerner and L. Steinberg (eds.), *Handbook of Adolescent Psychology.* New York: Wiley, 2004.

Darling, N., and Steinberg, L. "Parenting Style as Context: An Integrative Model." *Psychological Bulletin,* 1993, *113,* 487–496.

Gray, M., and Steinberg, L. "Unpacking Authoritative Parenting: Reassessing a Multidimensional Construct." *Journal of Marriage and the Family,* 1999, *61,* 574–587.

Hill, J. P. "Adapting to Menarche: Familial Control and Conflict." In M. R. Gunnar and W. A. Collins (eds.), *Development During the Transition to Adolescence: Minnesota Symposia on Child Psychology* (Vol. 21). Mahwah, N.J.: Erlbaum, 1988.

Maccoby, E. E., and Martin, J. "Socialization in the Context of the Family: Parent-Child Interaction." *Handbook of Child Psychology.* Vol. 4, E. M. Hetherington (ed.), *Socialization, Personality, and Social Development.* New York: Wiley, 1983.

Schaefer, E. W. "Children's Reports of Parental Behavior: An Inventory." *Child Development,* 1965, *36,* 413–424.

Silk, J., Morris, A., Kanaya, T., and Steinberg L. "Psychological Control and Autonomy Granting: Opposite Ends of a Continuum or Distinct Constructs?" *Journal of Research on Adolescence,* 2003, *13,* 113–128.

Silverberg, S., and Steinberg, L. "Adolescent Autonomy, Parent-Adolescent Conflict, and Parental Well-Being." *Journal of Youth and Adolescence,* 1987, *16,* 293–312.

Silverberg, S., and Steinberg, L. "Psychological Well-Being of Parents at Midlife: The Impact of Early Adolescent Children." *Developmental Psychology,* 1990, *26,* 658–666.

Steinberg, L. "Autonomy, Conflict, and Harmony in the Family Relationship." In S. Feldman and G. Elliot (eds.), *At the Threshold: The Developing Adolescent.* Cambridge, Mass.: Harvard University Press, 1990.

Steinberg, L., Elmen, J., and Mounts, N. "Authoritative Parenting, Psychosocial Maturity, and Academic Success Among Adolescents." *Child Development,* 1989, *60,* 1424–1436.

Steinberg, L., Lamborn, S., Dornbusch, S., and Darling, N. "Impact of Parenting Practices on Adolescent Achievement: Authoritative Parenting, School Involvement, and Encouragement to Succeed." *Child Development,* 1992, *63,* 1266–1281.

Steinberg, L., and Steinberg, W. *Crossing Paths: How Your Child's Adolescence Triggers Your Own Crisis.* New York: Simon & Schuster, 1994.

LAURENCE STEINBERG is the Distinguished University Professor and Laura H. Carnell Professor of Psychology at Temple University in Philadelphia.

Understanding parental influences and parent-adolescent relationships is difficult because individuals are involved in many activities and have varied goals. The chapters in this volume help address the complexities by focusing on variations in parental practices and domains of activities.

The Many Faces of Parenting

Elliot Turiel

A very important aim in the study of development is to understand interactions within families and the influences of parents on children. For a number of reasons, understanding family influences on development is also a difficult and complex task. One reason is that children spend a great deal of time with their parents in the context of many and varied activities. After all, children and parents spend time together day in and day out. It is also a difficult realm of study because the influences of many other activities on the part of parents and children need to be coordinated with direct family influences. Moreover, parents engage in many activities that might bear on their parenting. These include parents' relationships with each other, their work and their needs to support the family financially, their efforts at achieving personal goals in life, and their friendships and recreational activities. In addition to their relationships with parents, children interact with siblings, friends, and acquaintances and engage in activities in and out of school. Very important, family experiences occur while children's minds are developing and their world outside the family is continually expanding. And especially during adolescence, there is a great expansion of the individual's world, which renders the study of parental influences particularly difficult. Along these lines, it may also be the case that parents' ideas about children and parenting change through their experiences as parents.

Therefore, efforts to understand and explain parental influences on children and relationships between parents and children face the problem that it is very important to do so, but very difficult to do so given all the features that go into it. Quite understandably, early approaches (such as psychoanalytic and behaviorist theories) presumed that parents had an overriding influence on children, and rather general analyses were provided along positive and negative dimensions of parenting. I believe that this is the reason mothers especially (they spend more time than fathers with children) were said to be the cause of serious mental health problems in children (and later as adults). There was a time that the causes of autism and schizophrenia, as examples, were traced primarily to the actions of mothers. Now, of course, it is recognized that such explanations are highly simplistic and erroneous. I also believe that the broad sweep to parental influences is one of the reasons that some, also taking a broad sweep, claim that parents have a minimal effect on the social and personality development of their children. As an example, it has been asserted that the influences of genetics and peers (also broadly defined categories), rather than parents, are the main causes of development (Harris, 1995).

About fifty years ago, psychologists attempted to provide a little more specificity in characterizations of how parents relate to children by formulating categories that supposedly capture their general styles of child rearing. Parenting was portrayed through general orientations that parents presumably use to deal especially with misbehaviors. A set of often proposed categories included power assertion (predominant use of physical punishment), love withdrawal (use of social approval and disapproval), and induction (use of reasoning). Two questions are key regarding schemes that portray parents as mainly employing one general orientation in rearing or disciplining their children. Do the categories encompass the main ways parents relate to their children, and do parents mainly use one type? I believe that the answers to both questions are in the negative because broad categories of this sort fail to capture the different aspects of each general type (for example, different ways of using punishment, disapproval, or reasoning), parents' use of different practices for different situations and contexts, the ways parents are likely to combine different types of practices, and the bidirectional nature of the interactions (in the sense that parents and children engage in reciprocal interactions and influence each other).

It seems very unlikely that parents would respond in one general fashion regardless of the types of actions or desires on the part of their children in any given situation. As examples, most parents are likely to respond much more strongly, assertively, and with greater efforts at control if a child engages in actions that pose a danger to others or to the self or that are illegal (for example, theft) than if the actions have to do with manners, how to dress, or which play and leisure activities to pursue. In addition, actions that have to do with harm or illegalities are likely to be treated differently from actions that have to do with children's educational pursuits and goals, even when parents regard education as very important and it is taken seriously. Parents who are committed to guiding their children into particular activities—say, sports, arts, certain occupations, or religion—will be more assertive in those regards than other parents and that they themselves will be regarding other pursuits. Parents who think that a friend may lead their child in undesirable directions will react differently from the choice of a friend they simply do not like.

Most people do not approach the world in a general way that would allow them to be characterized through one type of template or orientation. People draw priorities, have preferences, and make distinctions in their choices and goals. Most people also have to adjust to life's circumstances. In turn, most people do not take a unitary approach to parenting. Surely most parents do not attempt to control all of their children's activities, but treat some in a less accepting or permissive way and others more permissively. Another aspect of this is that parents who live in a neighborhood they perceive to be dangerous or violent will treat certain actions more strictly than would parents in other neighborhoods. Thus, parents living in the midst of violence may be more vigilant about the friends or groups (such as gangs) their children choose (though the parents' own circumstance would have an effect). Some parents from ethnic or social class groups accorded fewer opportunities for economic advancement might stress schooling less than other choices, whereas other parents in the same groups may stress schooling.

These examples are meant to illustrate that parents make choices as to activities and directions to stress and therefore are likely to relate to their children in a variety of ways. Even if they believe in a particular approach to bringing up children, it is likely that circumstances result in much variability in parenting behaviors. Parenting is complicated by at least two other factors. One is that parents' relations with their children and the issues they pursue more or less vigorously change as their children become older. The changes can involve efforts at lesser and greater control and use of different types of control. As children become older, and especially during adolescence, parents usually start to recognize the need to allow more freedoms and self-direction. Nevertheless, issues may come up that result in efforts at greater parental control because of the seriousness of the consequences for the child or family. A second is that parents and children become involved in conflicts, and children sometimes overtly or covertly resist the parents' directives.

These considerations can be further examined through the results of a study on adolescents' judgments about deception of parents (Perkins, 2003). In this study, two groups of adolescents (one group between twelve and fourteen years old and the other between fifteen and seventeen years old) were presented with a set of hypothetical situations depicting adolescents who deceive parents (another set depicted deception of peers). One type of situation involved moral issues: parents tell an adolescent to act in ways that might be considered morally unjustifiable (not to befriend someone of different race or to confront physically someone who has been teasing him or her). Another type of situation involved issues that can be considered part of the personal realm (not to date someone the parents dislike or not to join a club since the parents think it is a waste of time). A third type involved personal matters with pragmatic considerations that can have serious consequences (to complete school work or not to ride a motorcycle).

The adolescents participating in the study were asked to judge the legitimacy of lying to parents by an adolescent in each of the situations. Their judgments differed by type of situation. The large majority of the adolescents thought it is legitimate to deceive parents with regard to the moral issues. They reasoned that deception was necessary to prevent injustice or harm. The majority also thought that deception was justified with regard to the personal issues. In this case, a greater proportion of the older group thought deception was legitimate than the younger group (though a majority did judge the deceptions legitimate). These patterns differed for parental directives about issues with pragmatic consequences in that the majority thought that deception was not legitimate, with more of the older than the younger group judging deception to be legitimate.

Two other sets of findings are revealing about the dynamics of parent-adolescent relationships. The first is that most of the participants thought that parental restrictions on the moral and personal issues were unjustified. By contrast, most thought that it is justifiable for parents to attempt to restrict the activities with the pragmatic consequences. Therefore, the perceived legitimacy of a parental restriction is associated with whether it is justified to deceive one's parents. However, it is not only the legitimacy of a restriction that bears on judgments about deception. The same study showed that most adolescents judged it unacceptable to deceive peers regarding the moral and personal issues, although they judged efforts by peers to impose such restrictions as unacceptable. A major difference between parent-child and peer relationships, as reflected in the reasons given by participants in the study, is the extent of equality and mutuality. Due to mutuality in their relationships, friends can confront each other about these matters. Since relationships with peers are unequal and parents are able to exert greater power and control, it is sometimes necessary to resort to deception. But not always. Deception of parents was judged less acceptable than deception of peers regarding the issues with pragmatic consequences.

Although the Perkins (2003) study assessed judgments about hypothetical situations, it is commonly known that adolescents do deceive their parents. Moreover, a survey in the year 2000 of over eight thousand high schools taken by the Josephson Institute of Ethics (Josephson, 2000) posed the general question, "Have you lied to your parents in the past 12 months?" The survey takers were stunned to find that 92 percent of the adolescents said that they had lied to their parents. Although members of the Josephson Institute regard the findings as indicative of the dire moral state of contemporary American adolescents, the findings actually demonstrate more about the multifaceted and complex nature of relationships with parents during the adolescent years. Perkins's research (2003) indicates that adolescents think that deception is undesirable but sometimes necessary for different reasons. And it appears that older adolescents are more likely than younger ones to see deception as necessary. The study also showed that the large majority of adolescents value honesty—in the abstract and in some situations. They judged lying to be wrong in response to general questions about it and in response to a situation in which an adolescent lies to parents or peers in order to cover up a misdeed.

To return to the problem I posed at the very start, it is difficult to study the important questions of parental influences on children and the nature of relationships between parents and children. Some of the difficulties stem from the variety of orientations parents might take regarding different types of issues, the associated reciprocity of interactions around such issues, and the changes in relationships, along with opposition and resistance, that occur especially during adolescence.

All the chapters in this volume represent efforts to account for the complexities of parent-adolescent relationships, starting with recognition of the difficulties in studying such relationships. In these chapters, we see attempts to account for differences in the realms or domains of activities and thereby analyses that do not treat parenting as unitary. Accounting for domains of judgment and associated social interactions brings with it the study of the perspectives of both parents and adolescents, as well as the types of interactions involved (agreement, negotiations, conflicts, and subversion, for example). The researchers examined issues demarcated by domains as approached by the adolescents and parents (not solely parents' beliefs and actions). Some of the studies discussed in this volume examined in part parental practices through the lens of categories formulated by Baumrind (1971), which can be construed as less global and to include greater distinctions than previous efforts to characterize parenting. The studies in this volume extend Baumrind's analyses in needed ways through the inclusion of the domain distinctions and by accounting for the perspectives of adolescents (and not only parents) in the interactions. The studies discussed here also begin to account for the social and economic conditions that might influence parent-adolescent interactions through the analyses of domains and ethnic or social class groups. And they share a concern with changes in parent-child relationships during adolescence.

The research discussed by Barber, Maughan, and Olsen in Chapter One bears the least on distinctions among the moral, conventional, and personal domains. They draw important distinctions in parenting through the categories of behavioral control and psychological control. These findings demonstrate that there are both stability and change during adolescence, as well as different perceptions between parents and adolescents. For instance, expressions of physical affection and the limits set by parents decline with the child's age. Yet changes were not observed in parental use of psychological control. The differing perceptions of parents and adolescents were in the realms of parents' knowledge and monitoring of the activities of adolescents.

Parents thought that they knew and monitored less as the adolescents grew older—but the adolescents did not see it that way.

The research discussed in Chapters Two through Four examined distinctions in domains of activities. The authors of those chapters share with Barber, Maughan, and Olsen the view that autonomy and a sense of self are significant aspects of adolescent development that can be interfered with by too much parental psychological control or too much intrusion into their decisions and activities. However, the studies discussed in this volume show that the effects of excessive control by parents on matters of autonomy or the development of a sense of self are linked to particular types of issues and activities: those in the personal domain. Parent-adolescent relationships around issues in the moral domain seem to be an entirely different matter. Darling, Cumsille, and Peña-Alampay in Chapter Four report that their pilot research in the United States, Chile, and the Philippines demonstrated that adolescents did not see moral issues as a source of conflict with parents. That pilot work is consistent with findings from studies by Smetana, Crean, and Campione-Bass in Chapter Three in several countries and with African American and European American samples. In the moral domain, there is general agreement between parents and adolescents, as well as acceptance of the legitimacy of parents to regulate adolescents' activities. This means that autonomy, the development of a sense of self, and overcontrol or overly restrictive behaviors are not relevant to the moral domain (and to some extent, conventional and prudential matters).

It is primarily issues surrounding the personal domain that are seen to affect the development of autonomy. However, the classification of personal issues, as related to parenting, is not straightforward because other factors come into play. A salient set of factors that bear on how parents will relate to a child has to do with timing. To understand how this is the case, it is helpful to think in terms of how a parent would approach an issue as it applies to a (competent) adult. There are issues that most parents would classify as personal, but not necessarily for people of all ages because of the idea of physical or psychological readiness. Parents may judge that an activity is under personal jurisdiction but that people below a certain age ought not to be engaging in the activity. For illustrative purposes, consider the example of learning how to drive an automobile. Most parents will think that it is up to the individual to decide whether and when to learn to drive. (I leave aside for now prudential and pragmatic issues of knowing how to drive safely and the need to drive in order to achieve educational or occupational goals.) It is up to the individual, up to a point, to decide when to learn how to drive. However, it is not up to a ten-year-old, for instance, but it is up to a twenty-year-old. It may not be up to a sixteen-year-old in a crowded urban area, but it may be up to a fourteen- or sixteen-year-old in a sparsely populated rural area.

There may be little conflict over the age of learning to drive (especially since it is legally prescribed in most states), but these types of conflict do occur over many personal issues when parents and adolescents disagree over timing, as is well documented in the research discussed in this volume. One of the main sources of conflict over personal issues that would not usually be seen with regard to learning to drive a car is the asynchrony between parents' and adolescents' views as to when to expand boundaries of personal jurisdiction. The findings indicate that parents often lag behind adolescents in this regard. Adolescents do view the boundaries of their personal jurisdiction to be expanding, but parents are sometimes unwilling to grant them the expansion quite yet. The dynamics around these different views of the boundaries of personal jurisdiction do not only bear on whether adolescents get to do what they want. The personal domain, as conceptualized in this volume, has a deeper meaning connected to the development of self and a sense of identity. For these reasons, adolescents with parents who are unwilling to sufficiently grant personal jurisdiction and an expansion of its boundaries are more likely to experience psychological difficulties. The research indicates that the psychological effects of parental "overcontrol" is not limited to one cultural group (that is, it is documented for European Americans, African Americans, and Japanese) and does not apply to all realms. Overcontrol does not seem relevant for symptoms of psychological difficulties for moral or conventional matters. The research findings on maladjustment reported by Nucci, Hasebe, and Lins-Dyer, as well as by Smetana and Daddis (2002), forcefully demonstrate the significance of various types of personal issues in the lives of adolescents. Parents may view matters like dress, recreation, and friendship choices as ones they can control without harmful consequences since they are not earthshaking matters. From the perspective of adolescents, however, these (and many more) are matters central in their lives and in forming a sense of personal agency.

I believe it is of great relevance to relationships between parents and adolescents that each sometimes differently interprets the time in life that personal boundaries should be extended. More generally, differences in interpretations of certain events are a major source of tension. This is why issues referred to as multifaceted or mixed or involving overlap of domains are also sources of conflict. Research shows that mixed issues, as well as straightforward moral and conventional issues, are very much a part of the events that children and adolescents experience in social settings (see Turiel, 2002). As discussed in Chapters One through Four, issues that combine personal and conventional or prudential considerations are another source of disagreement and conflict. Most likely this is because issues that combine more than one domain readily allow the parents to focus on one aspect, such as the prudential, and the adolescent to focus another, such as the personal. This is not to say that parents or adolescents are unaware of the different components involved. It is to say that multifaceted events are sufficiently ambiguous to provide contexts for multiple interpretations.

Consider again the example of when to learn how to drive, with the inclusion of pragmatic components. If parents perceive that their adolescent is not driving safely (for example, the adolescent is seen as taking risks), they will treat the activity as one that requires their surveillance and efforts at controlling when and how he or she drives. By contrast, the adolescent may believe that his or her driving is not unsafe (perhaps that the parents are too cautious) and resist their efforts. Similarly, if parents believe that their adolescent needs to learn to drive by a certain age because it is a necessary skill for success in realms like education and work, they might attempt to guide the time he or she learns to drive. By contrast, the adolescent may believe that he or she can achieve educational and occupational goals without knowing how to drive. Different perceptions regarding different components from different domains can and often result in disagreements between parents and adolescents.

Another value of the chapters in this volume is that they go well beyond stereotypes about cultures and do not rely on facile explanations of type of parenting as due to their cultural orientations. Analyses of cultures and their influences on children's development, like early analyses of parenting, too often rely on the proposition that cultures can be distinguished by general orientations to self and social interactions on the dimensions of individualism (where the person, independence, and boundaries between people are central) and collectivism (where the group, interdependence, and lack of boundaries among people are central). In that framework, it would be expected that the cultural orientation would result in how parents relate to their children and what they attempt to convey to them. Regarding issues discussed extensively in this volume, it would be expected that in the so-called individualistic cultures (usually Western), parents would emphasize the self, agency, and the sanctity of freedoms and the personal domain. Parents in so-called collectivist cultures would downplay the personal in favor of interdependence and shared activities.

The dynamics of relationships between parents and adolescents, with struggles over boundaries of personal jurisdiction, cannot simply be explained through general cultural orientations. The analyses in this volume avoid the easy attribution of culture to parent-adolescent interactions in two ways. One is through close examination of relationships from both perspectives. The second is by deeper consideration of the environmental conditions of different groups (ethnic and social class) within society. Darling, Cumsille, and Peña-Alampay report findings from the United States, Chile, and the Philippines confirming that parents and adolescents draw the domain distinctions. They also found that in each nation, adolescents come to regard more issues under their legitimate control and fewer under parental control as they grow older. In each nation, autonomy and a sense of self are part of the process of development during adolescence. Along with many studies of other aspects of social judgments (Turiel, 2002), these studies show that cultures cannot be stereotyped on the dimensions that some associate with individualism and collectivism.

Nevertheless, parents in the United States seem to grant grater autonomy to adolescents at earlier ages than parents in Chile and the Philippines; however, in Chile and the Philippines, there is greater discrepancy between parent and adolescent views since parents grant autonomy later than adolescents desire it. Darling, Cumsille, and Peña-Alampay discuss interesting patterns of similarities and differences among the three nations that cannot be readily attributed to their culture. One of the findings of national differences is that Filipino parents were more likely than Chilean parents to set rules and that Filipino adolescents believe it is legitimate for parents to do so. In a seemingly paradoxical finding, the Filipino adolescents reported more conflicts and disagreements with their parents than did adolescents from Chile. However, the finding is not paradoxical if we keep in mind that the adolescents are concerned with maintaining their autonomy and do strive for what Nucci, Hasebe, and Lins-Dyer refer to as a personal zone. In the Filipino context, this striving is manifested in the emergence of conflicts and arguments even though parents and adolescents espouse legitimacy of rule setting and obedience.

The findings discussed in this volume show that there are similarities between certain groups in different cultures, as well as differences between groups within cultures. The findings point to the importance of social, economic, and environmental conditions in parental practices. In particular, the dangers, risks, and challenges facing groups in vulnerable positions in society influence parents' relationships with their adolescents. Across cultures or nations, groups are at risk because they are denied opportunities, face dangers, and find themselves in subordinate positions in the social hierarchy. Lower-class Brazilian parents of children are more restrictive than Brazilian middle-class parents (though by the time the children were sixteen year old, there were no class differences). Also, lower-class Brazilian mothers saw themselves as exerting control over their daughters because of the risks their children faced. Probably in an accurate way, lower-class Brazilian girls thought that their mothers exerted greater control than did middle-class girls.

These findings indicate that it is not only characteristics of parents, as individuals or as shaped by their culture, that make for parental practices. It is an interactive process in that parents act in accord with how they perceive the world. They make judgments about what children need to do to be safe and successful. African American parents in the United States are attuned to these issues, just as are lower-class Brazilian parents and parents in urban Hong Kong (as discussed by Smetana, Crean, and Campione-Barr). Would these parents relate to their adolescents differently if they did not face dangers in their neighborhoods, believe that their group had educational and occupational opportunities equal to other groups, or lived in a society without racial discrimination? The likely answer is that in many ways, they would act differently, since it has been shown that middle-class parents often grant greater autonomy in personal realms to adolescents.

We must keep in mind, however, that there are variations in how parents and adolescents interact within each of these groups. The domains of activity, life's circumstances, goals in many realms of life, and risks and dangers in the world (faced also by middle-class parents) all contribute to variations in the ways parents relate to their children. The chapters in this volume, by seeking to account for these features, provide grounding for the complex and difficult problem of understanding parent-adolescent relationships in ways that do not rely on global or unitary perspectives on parenting.

References

Baumrind, D. "Current Patterns of Parental Authority." *Developmental Psychology Monographs*, 1971, 4(1, part 2).

Harris, J. R. "Where Is the Child's Environment? A Group Socialization Theory of Development." *Psychological Review*, 1995, *102*, 458–489.

Josephson Institute of Ethics. "Report Card on the Ethics of American Youth" (www.josephsoninstitute.org). Oct. 16, 2000.

Perkins, S. A. "Adolescent Reasoning About Lying in Close Relationships." Unpublished doctoral dissertation, University of California, Berkeley, 2003.

Smetana, J. G., and Daddis, C. "Domain-Specific Antecedents of Psychological Control and Parental Monitoring: The Role of Parenting Beliefs and Practices." *Child Development*, 2002, *73*(2), 563–580.

Turiel, E. *The Culture of Morality: Social Development, Context, and Conflict.* Cambridge: Cambridge University Press, 2002.

ELLIOT TURIEL is Chancellor's Professor of Education and associate dean at the University of California, Berkeley.

INDEX

Domain theory: ambiguities in, 64, 65–66, 68; aspects of, 17–18, 32–33; assumption of, 68; consistency with, 54; limitations of, 76–77; premise of, 65; reasoning in, 53; and the vicissitudes of conflict, 73–74. *See also* Conventional issues; Moral issues; Overlapping issues; Personal issues; Prudential issues

Dornbusch, S. M., 6, 17, 21, 24, 39, 40, 74

Drug and alcohol use, adolescents engaged in, view of, on decision making, 40

Early childhood, conflict evident in, 19
Education level, of African American mothers, and legitimacy of parental authority, 34, 36
Eisenberg, N., 7, 8, 11, 12
Elmen, J., 71
Equality, extent of, 82
Erickson, L. D., 7
Ethnicity/race: in autonomy study, 50; and boundaries of the personal domain, 33; and knowledge/monitoring, 12, 13; and level of parental control, 28; in Ogden Youth and Family Project, 8. *See also specific ethnic and racial groups*
European Americans, 39–40, 42, 84
Expectation issues, parental, 53–54, 55

Factor analyses, 61
Family decision making: assessment of, 21, 38; and autonomy, 39–41
Family Decision Making Checklist, 21
Family influences, complexity surrounding, on development, 79
Family structure, and limit setting, 12
Fathers: behavioral control of, 12; domains regulated by, 64; psychological control of, 12; support from, 11; varied patterns of, 13
Filipino adolescents and parents, 48, 49–56, 57, 84, 86
Filipino culture, values in, 49
Fletcher, A. C., 56
Flexible parenting style, 18, 63
Franklin, A. J., 36
Friendship issues, multifaceted, 35, 36, 37, 38
Fuligni, A. J., 33, 42

Gaines, C., 18, 19, 20, 23, 34, 42
Galambos, N. L., 66
Ge, X., 5, 8
Gender, and legitimacy of parental authority, 34, 56
Gender socialization, notions of, in the U.S., 14
Genetics, influence of, 80
Gonzales, N., 40, 43
Good-enough parents, 62
Goodnow, J. J., 31
Gray, M., 6, 72
Grusec, J. E., 31
Guerra, N., 40

Hall, G. E., 11
Hames, K., 50
Harmon, E., 19, 27, 66
Harris, J. D., 7, 8, 11, 12
Harris, J. R., 80
Harter, S., 40
Hasebe, Y., 1, 2, 17, 19, 21, 26, 39, 63, 65, 67, 72, 76, 85, 87
Head, M. R., 31
Hierarchical linear model (HLM) analyses, 51, 54, 56
Hierarchical regression analyses, 38
Hill, J. P., 73
Hiraga, Y., 40, 43
Hoff, E., 36
Honesty, value of, 83
Human development, transcendent aspects of, acknowledging, 27. *See also Developmental entries*

Ideal Control Index (IC), 21, 26
Idealized control, 22–23, 24, 26
Identity, 18, 19, 33, 37, 41, 72–73
Immigrant adolescents and parents, Mexican, 24–25
Immigrant status, 24
Independence, interfering with, 19
Individualism: and collectivism, cross-cultural comparison of, 48–49; defining, 86
Individualistic cultures: extending adolescent-parent dynamic from, 19, 20; stereotype and reality of, 27, 86–87
Individuation process, 73
Induction, 80
Inflated outcomes, 63
Instability of parental support, 11–12
Intake instrument, 26

Back Issue/Subscription Order Form

Copy or detach and send to:
Jossey-Bass, A Wiley Imprint, 989 Market Street, San Francisco CA 94103-1741

Call or fax toll-free: Phone 888-378-2537 6:30AM —3PM PST; Fax 888-481-2665

Back Issues: Please send me the following issues at $29 each
(Important: please include series initials and issue number, such as CD99.)

_____

_____

_____

$ _____ Total for single issues

$ _____ SHIPPING CHARGES: SURFACE   Domestic   Canadian
                                    First Item $5.00 $6.00
                                    Each Add'l Item $3.00 $1.50
                 For next-day and second-day delivery rates, call the number listed above.

Subscriptions   Please ___ start ___ renew my subscription to *New Directions
                for Child and Adolescent Development* for the year 2 _____ at the
                following rate:

                U.S.   ___ Individual $90   ___ Institutional $205
                Canada   ___ Individual $90   ___ Institutional $245
                All Others   ___ Individual $114   ___ Institutional $279

$ _____ Total single issues and subscriptions (Add appropriate sales tax for
                 your state for single issue orders. No sales tax for U.S. subscriptions.
                 Canadian residents, add GST for subscriptions and single issues.)

___ Payment enclosed (U.S. check or money order only)
___ VISA ___ MC ___ AmEx # _____ Exp. Date _____

Signature _____ Day Phone _____
___ Bill Me (U.S. institutional orders only. Purchase order required.)

Purchase order # _____
                  Federal Tax ID13559302   GST 89102 8052

Name _____

Address _____

_____

Phone _____ E-mail _____

For more information about Jossey-Bass, visit our Web site at www.josseybass.com

NEW DIRECTIONS FOR
CHILD AND ADOLESCENT DEVELOPMENT
IS NOW AVAILABLE ONLINE AT WILEY INTERSCIENCE

What is Wiley InterScience?

Wiley InterScience is the dynamic online content service from John Wiley & Sons delivering the full text of over 300 leading scientific, technical, medical, and professional journals, plus major reference works, the acclaimed Current Protocols laboratory manuals, and even the full text of select Wiley print books online.

What are some special features of Wiley InterScience?

Wiley Interscience Alerts is a service that delivers table of contents via e-mail for any journal available on Wiley InterScience as soon as a new issue is published online.
EarlyView is Wiley's exclusive service presenting individual articles online as soon as they are ready, even before the release of the compiled print issue. These articles are complete, peer-reviewed, and citable.
CrossRef is the innovative multi-publisher reference linking system enabling readers to move seamlessly from a reference in a journal article to the cited publication, typically located on a different server and published by a different publisher.

How can I access Wiley InterScience?

Visit http://www.interscience.wiley.com.

Guest Users can browse Wiley InterScience for unrestricted access to journal tables of contents and article abstracts, or use the powerful search engine.
Registered Users are provided with a *Personal Home Page* to store and manage customized alerts, searches, and links to favorite journals and articles. Additionally, Registered Users can view free online sample issues and preview selected material from major reference works.
Licensed Customers are entitled to access full-text journal articles in PDF, with select journals also offering full-text HTML.

How do I become an Authorized User?

Authorized Users are individuals authorized by a paying Customer to have access to the journals in Wiley InterScience. For example, a university that subscribes to Wiley journals is considered to be the Customer.
Faculty, staff and students authorized by the university to have access to those journals in Wiley InterScience are Authorized Users. Users should contact their library for information on which Wiley journals they have access to in Wiley InterScience.

THE PRICE OF NEGLECT

The Price
of Neglect

A.W. Tozer

Compiled by
Harry Verploegh

WingSpread Publishers
Camp Hill, Pennsylvania

WingSpread Publishers
Camp Hill, Pennsylvania
www.wingspreadpublishers.com

A division of Zur Ltd.

The Price of Neglect
ISBN: 978-1-60066-040-5
© 1991 by Zur Ltd.

Previously published by Christian Publications, Inc.
First Christian Publications Edition 1991
First WingSpread Publishers Edition 2010

Scripture taken from
the Holy Bible: King James Version

CONTENTS

FOREWORD

Anointed for
This Generation

We know both from the Scriptures and from the history of the church that times of spiritual and moral declension are sure to come. It may be, as with us today, in the form of secularism, a muting or outright compromise of biblical truths, carnal worship or life styles practically identical with that of the world.

In such critical times God in His providence chose and "anointed" some person with a divine intuition, a built-in enablement to detect and decisively refuse whatever is basically incompatible with true biblical doctrine, spiritual worship and morality no matter who presents it or how it is set forth.

Such a divinely gifted person with consummate clarity, pointedness and skill calls God's true children to not follow the trends but to return to those teachings that are dear to the heart of God and to a transformation in the morals of persons and congregations.

Dr. A.W. Tozer, without question, had such an "anointing" for this generation. As an articulate preacher and perspicuous writer he assumed the role of a reverent forecaster. His so accurate description of unseemly religious and moral conditions and where they were leading the church are black facts that make one wonder about the "religion" in the evangelical church of our day.

His prophetic soul was impatient and even intractable in the face of the evangelical community's growing moral stupidity coupled with religious emotionalism and easy egoism. He decried that ". . . the whole evangelical world is to a large extent unfavorable to healthy Christianity. And I am not thinking of modernism either. I mean rather the Bible-believing crowd that bears the name of orthodoxy."

Nor was he quiescent when there arose those who claimed to have access to deeper teachings, to more esoteric truth, to a more reasonable theology, or to a more-compatible-with-the-times form of worship. More than any other, he dealt faithfully with sin and religious sham, rebuking anything that didn't square with Scripture. Also, with the illuminating flash of a mind literally steeped in the Word of God and exercised by the Holy Spirit, he was equally able to reveal the beauties of many a hidden truth and to so magnify the person and work of Christ that his auditors were awestruck.

Perhaps nothing finer could be said of Dr. Tozer than that he belonged to the great race of prophets and apostles. By nearly unanimous voice evangelical commentators have conferred on him the title, "The 20th Century Prophet."

Though he passed away in 1963, through this man's voluminous writings God continues to lay His hand on our minds and hearts. He possessed an aspiration and an inspiration and a spiritual aura which still influences a vast and admiring readership. While he lived, those of us who were privileged to know him well felt that here was a man who came forth from the inner place with its fragrance about him, though he himself seemed quite unconscious of it. This fragrance by divine alchemy is transmitted to us in his writings, of which this book is but a sample.

Probably no person now living is as well qualified to prepare a book of this nature as Harry Verploegh. Because of his long and close association with Dr. Tozer as friend, confidant and faithful partner, he has been able to sense what was in his mind and therefore make a splendid representative selection of his writings—excerpts compiled from his thought-provoking editorials and heart-searching sermons. Here then are vignettes of Dr. Tozer's thought which exerted such a wide-ranging influence and made such a profound impression on all sorts and conditions of people. His transparent sincerity, the literary charm of his style, his peculiar ability to communicate, his persuasive power in presenting Christ in the glory of His person, and in the fullness and fruitfulness of His work are all here for the reader to enjoy.

Louis L. King (d. 2004)
President, (1978-1987)
The Christian and Missionary Alliance

The Price of Neglect

Plato has somewhere said that in a demo-cratic society the price wise men pay for ne-glecting politics is to be ruled by unwise men. *[AMEN!!]*

This observation is so patently true that no one who values his reputation for clear thinking is likely to contest it.

In America, for instance, there are millions of plain men and women, decent, honest and peace loving, who take their blessings for granted and make no effort to assure the continuance of our free society. These persons are without doubt far in the majority. They constitute the main body of our population, but for all their numbers they are not going to determine the direction our country will go in the next few years. Their weakness lies *[weakness lies in passivity]* in their passivity. They sit back and allow radicals and those in the minority but who shout the loudest to set the course for the future. If this continues much longer we have no assurance that we can retain that liberty which was once purchased for us at such appalling cost.

The price good and sober Christians pay for doing nothing is to be led by those highly vocal minorities whose only qualifications for leadership are an overweening ambition and a loud voice. And there have always been and always will be such persons in the congregations of the saints. They know least and talk most, while sane and godly men too often give up leadership to them rather than to resist them. Later these same docile souls may shake their heads and lament their captivity. But by that time it is too late.

Within the circles of evangelical Christianity itself there has arisen in the last few years dangerous and dismaying trends away from true Bible Christianity. A spirit has been introduced which is surely not the Spirit of Christ, methods employed which are wholly carnal, objectives adopted which have not one line of Scripture to support them, a level of conduct accepted which is practically identical with that of the world—and yet scarcely one voice has been raised in opposition. And this in spite of the fact that the Bible-honoring followers of Christ lament among themselves the dangerous, wobbly course things are taking.

So radically is the essential spirit and content of orthodox Christianity changing these days under the vigorous leadership of undiscerning religionists that, if the trend is not stopped, what is called

Christianity will soon be something altogether other than the faith of our fathers. We'll have only Bible words left. Bible religion will have perished from wounds received in the house of her friends.

The times call for a Spirit-baptized and articulate orthodoxy. They whose souls have been illuminated by the Holy Ghost must arise and under God assume leadership. There are those among us whose hearts can discern between the true and the false, whose spiritual sense of smell enables them to detect the spurious afar off, who have the blessed gift of *knowing*. Let such as these arise and be heard. Who knows but the Lord may return and leave a blessing behind Him?

Do I look different than the world?
Do I speake " ly " "
Do I act " " "
Do I love " "

CHAPTER

2

The Christian Funeral
Needs a Reformation

We have long been of the opinion that for
the blood-washed Christian the worst
thing about dying is the funeral. Even among gospel Christians the funeral obsequies have degener-
ated into a gloomy ordeal that leaves everybody
miserable for days. The only one not affected by the
general heaviness that hangs over everything is the
servant of God who has died and in whose honor
the service is held. He has gone where the wicked
cease from troubling and the weary be at rest. The
minister and the undertaker, however, see to it that
those who remain are neither untroubled nor at
rest.

An odd contradiction exists here, for dolefulness is just what everybody is trying to avoid. Every effort is made to create the impression that the deceased is not really dead, and that the cemetery is not a graveyard at all but a pleasant park where everything is bright and full of cheer. Strangely enough, in spite of this obvious effort, the average funeral (even the Christian funeral) succeeds only in accenting the presence of death all the more. The dimmed lights, the low music, the smell of cut flowers, the unnatural tones of the minister and his slow march ahead of the coffin all contribute to the feeling of utter futility with which the service is charged.

We can't beat death by setting it to music. The instinct of the human heart is too strong to be cheated by little well-meant attempts to turn away its thoughts from the serious business of death and dying. Death is a solemn fact. Only unbelief or the insensibility caused by sin prevent the funeral of an unsaved man from being an agony of terror for his unsaved relatives. The honest minister can bring to the funeral of a lost man no real words of hope for the deceased. For the living there is hope, and the minster may do well to point them to the Savior, but if he has a proper regard for the sacredness of his office he will not give the living false hope concerning the dead.

The basic spirituality of any group of professed Christians may be discovered by observing the conduct of its advocates when faced with the harsh necessity of death. Where there is abounding gospel assurance among believers the funeral invariably takes on the air of a celebration rather than of a lamentation. Where that assurance is lacking, the whole atmosphere reveals it, however bravely the minister may quote, "There is no death, what seems so is transition." Where various ecclesiastical wires are pulled in an effort to secure last minute favors for the departed, where every attempt is made to placate death by timid posturing and ingratiating genuflections, we may be sure that the true gospel light has not shined. For a ransomed man knows how to die without crawling, and ransomed men know how to keep their poise in the presence of death.

The early Methodists enjoyed a degree of spiritual victory that lifted them above sorrow at the passing of their brethren. One of their funeral songs, for instance, ran like this:

Hosanna to Jesus on high!
    Another has entered her rest:
Another has 'scaped to the sky,
    And lodged in Immanuel's breast;
The soul of our sister is gone
    To heighten the triumph above;
Exalted to Jesus' throne,
    And clasped in the arms of his love.

Another song often heard when the Methodists lay away their beloved dead was this:

Weep not for a brother deceased;
    Our loss is his infinite gain;
A soul out of prison released,

And freed from its bodily chain;
With songs let us follow his flight,
And mount with his spirit above.
Escaped to the mansions of light,
And lodged in the Eden above.

How inferior the songs we sing today at the graves of our Christian dead. The note of joyous triumph is gone. The whole mood reflects the plaintive hopelessness of paganism. By our conduct at the funeral of those who sleep in Jesus we effectually cancel out the testimony they gave while they lived. It is time for a change.

We share with other believers the hope that for many of us the return of Christ may circumvent death and project us into the Immaculate Presence without the necessity of dying. But if not, then let there be no gloomy faces among the few that gather to pay their last regards. We lived with the Resurrection in our heart and died in the Everlasting Arms. Hosanna! There's no room there for lamentation.

"I have observed," said the old historian, "that these Christians die well." A Christian can die well because he is the only one who dares to die at all. The lost man cannot afford to die, and that he must die is his infinite woe. A Christian dares to die because his Savior has died and risen. Let us renounce paganism at our funerals and die as we lived, like Christians.

We Must Have True Faith

To many Christians Christ is little more than an idea, or at best an ideal; He is not a fact. Millions of professed believers talk as if He were real and act as if He were not. And always our actual position is to be discovered by the way we act, not by the way we talk.

We can prove our faith by our committal to it, and in no other way. Any belief that does not command the one who has it is not a real belief; it is a pseudo-belief only. And it might shock some of us profoundly if we were brought suddenly face to face with our beliefs and forced to test them in the fires of practical living.

Many of us Christians have become extremely skillful in arranging our lives so as to admit the truth of Christianity without being embarrassed by its implications. We fix things so that we can get on well enough without divine aid, while at the same time ostensibly seeking it. We boast in the Lord but watch carefully that we never get caught depending on Him. "The heart is deceitful above all things, and desperately wicked: who can know it?" (Jeremiah 17:9)?

Pseudo-faith always arranges a way out to serve in case God fails it. Real faith knows only one way and gladly allows itself to be stripped of any second ways or makeshift substitutes. For true faith, it is either God or total collapse. And not since Adam first stood up on the earth has God failed a single man or woman who trusted Him.

The man of pseudo-faith will fight for his verbal creed but refuse flatly to allow himself to get into a predicament where his future must depend upon that creed being true. He always provides himself with secondary ways of escape so he will have a way out if the roof caves in.

What we need very badly these days is a company of Christians who are prepared to trust God as completely now as they know they must do at the last day. For each of us the time is surely coming when we shall have nothing but God. Health and wealth and friends and hiding places will all be swept away and we shall have only God. To the man of pseudo-faith that is a terrifying thought, but to real faith it is one of the most comforting thoughts the heart can entertain.

It would be a tragedy indeed to come to the place where we have no other but God and find that we had not been trusting God at all during the days of our earthly sojourn. It would be better to *invite* God now to remove every false trust, to disengage our hearts from all secret hiding places and to bring us out into the open where we can discover for ourselves whether or not we really trust Him. That is a harsh cure for our troubles, but it is a sure one. Gentler cures may be too weak to do the work. And time is running out on us.

Lyric Theology

R eligious productions which come into being during times of great spiritual blessing
are to be valued above those which appear during
times of spiritual decline. Especially is this true if
the production is a fair reflection of the spiritual
state which prevails at the time it is written.

Examples are not hard to find. Take for instance
the hymnody that sprang up around the Method-
ist revival of the nineteenth century. One hymnal
put out by the Methodists lies at hand as we write.
It was published in the year 1849. It contains 1,148
hymns, 553 of them written by Charles Wesley,
and the amazing thing about the book is that
there is hardly an inferior hymn in it. One quality
which marks the hymns is the large measure of
sound doctrine that is found in them. Quite a
complete course in theology could be gotten from

the hymnal alone without recourse to any other textbook.

The Holy Spirit was upon the Methodists in fullness of grace, and they sang of God and Christ and the Scriptures and of the mysteries and joys of redemption personally experienced. The hymnal is lyric theology, a theology that had been strained through the pores of the men and women who wrote and sang their joyous songs. The hymns are warm with the breath of worshipers, a breath that may still be detected fragrant upon them after the passing of a century.

Lay this hymnal beside almost any of the productions of the last fifty years and compare them. The differences will be found to be pronounced, and to the devout soul more than a little depressing. The last half-century has been for the most part a period of religious decline, and the hymnody which it has produced has expressed its low spiritual state. With the coming of the great religious campaigns, with their popular evangelists and their mass appeal, religious singing started on a long trip down, a trip which from all appearances has not yet ended. Experience took the place of theology in popular singing. Writers became more concerned with joy bells than with the blood of sprinkling. Ballad tunes displaced the graver and more serious type of melody. The whole spiritual mood declined and the songs expressed the mood faithfully.

At the risk of being written off as hopelessly outmoded, we venture to give it as our studied opinion that about the only good thing in the average modern songbook is the section of great hymns which most of them carry in the back—hymns which for the most part were written when the Church was at her flood and which are included now as a gesture of respect to the past, and rarely sung.

Hobab's Eyes

During the early days of the wilderness journey of the Israelites an odd and significant transaction took place between Moses and an in-law named Hobab. *— his brother-in-law*

> And Moses said unto Hobab . . . We are journeying unto the place of which the LORD said, I will give it you: come thou with us, and we will do thee good . . . And he said unto him, I will not go; but I will depart to mine own land, and to my kindred. And he said, Leave us not, I pray thee; forasmuch as thou knowest how we are to encamp in the wilderness, and thou mayest be to us instead of eyes. And it shall be, if thou go with us, yea, it shall be, that what goodness the LORD shall do unto us, the same will we do unto thee. (Numbers 10:29-32)

Imagine! Moses hired a guide to lead Israel through the wilderness! The circumstances being what they were, this seems almost incredible, but Moses was a man capable of making mistakes like the rest of us. And hiring Hobab was a serious mistake. Here is why.

God had already told Moses that He himself would lead Israel into the promised land. "Behold, I send an Angel before thee, to keep thee in the way, and to bring thee into the place which I have prepared" (Exodus 23:20). God had also provided the wondrous cloud and fire to lead them (Numbers 9:15-23). Furthermore, in the very chapter that tells of Moses' effort to enlist Hobab's aid it is written, "And they departed from the mount of the LORD three days' journey: and the ark of the covenant of the LORD went before them in the three days' journey, to search out a resting place for them" (Numbers 10:33). So through the divinely appointed angel and by means of the ark and the cloudy pillar *God Himself was guiding Israel through the wilderness.* What need then had they of Hobab's eyes?

Hobab was not to blame for his part in this strange doing, but his presence added nothing to the safety of the marching army; and there is reason to believe that he may have been a spiritual stumbling block both to Moses and to the nation of Israel. The more they trusted to Hobab the less they trusted in God. And that was bad for Israel.

The Church also has her appointed Guide to lead her in her earthly journey. "But the Comforter, which is the Holy Ghost, whom the Father will send in my name, he shall teach you all things, and bring all things to your remembrance, whatsoever I have said unto you" (John 14:26). "For as many as are led by the Spirit of God, they are the sons of God" (Romans 8:14). These and a wealth of other Scriptures assure us that we are under the direct care of the Holy Spirit. Safety and fruitfulness require only that we accept the leadership of God. Blessing lies in the way of submission and obedience.

What need do we have of Hobab's eyes? Surely none at all. Yet the Church has a whole army of Hobabs to which it looks eagerly for guidance and leadership. That Hobab has no place in the divine plan never seems to matter at all. That Hobab is an intruder, that his eyes are not sharp enough to search out the path, that he is altogether superfluous and actually in the way is passed over by almost everyone. God seems so far away, the Bible is such an old book, faith makes such heavy demands upon our flesh, and Hobab is so near at hand and so real and easy to lean on so we act like men of earth instead of like men of heaven, and Hobab gets the job.

Now, who is Hobab? and how can we identify him? The answer is easy. Hobab is anything gratuitously introduced into the holy work of God which does not have biblical authority for its existence. At first this new thing may seem innocent enough and even look like an improvement over the biblical pattern; and because it is new it is sure to catch on fast and spread quickly among the churches. We Christians are soon playing "follow the leader," trotting along docilely behind Hobab and justifying his presence by appealing to his popularity. Anyone as popular as Hobab cannot be wrong, no matter how far he may be from the Word of God.

Hobab is not an individual. He is whatever takes our attention from the cloud and fire; he is whatever causes us to lean less heavily upon God and look less trustfully to the guiding Spirit. Each one of us must look out for him in our own life and in our church. And when we discover him we must get rid of him right away.

CHAPTER

6

On Brother Lawrence

One of the purest souls ever to live on this fallen planet was Nicholas Herman, that simple-hearted Christian known throughout the world as Brother Lawrence. He wrote very little, but what he wrote has seemed to several generations of Christians to be so rare and so beautiful as to deserve a place near the top among the world's great books of devotion. So well is he established in the affection of spiritual souls of all denominations and every shade of Christian thought that it is hardly too much to say that the expressions of an adverse opinion of Brother Lawrence may be taken as evidence that the critic is either a victim of his own prejudices, or is too engrossed with this world even to understand the spirit of a man as heavenly-minded as he.

Early in his life Brother Lawrence found Christ as his own Saviour and Lord and entered into what he called "the unspeakable riches of God and of Jesus Christ." He was a common cook but he learned to turn the modest service into a kind of worship. "We can do little things for God," he said. "I turn the cake that is frying on the pan for love of Him, and that done, if there is nothing else to call me, I prostrate myself in worship before Him who has given me grace to work. Afterwards I rise happier than a king."

He spent his long life walking in the presence of His Lord, and when he came to die there was no need for any particular change in his occupation. At the last hour someone asked him what was going on in his thoughts as death approached. He replied simply: "I am doing what I shall do through all eternity—blessing God, praising God, adoring God, giving Him the love of my whole heart. It is our one business, my brethren, to worship Him and love Him without thought of anything else."

The writings of Brother Lawrence are the ultimate in simplicity. His teachings knew very little variety, and consisted mostly of a few great ideas woven like costly threads to make a pattern of great beauty.

Our Low Level of Moral Enthusiasm: Part I

W ere some watcher or holy one from the bright world above to come among us for a time with the power to diagnose the spiritual ills of church people there is one entry which I am quite sure would appear on the vast majority of his reports: *Definite evidence of chronic spiritual lassitude; level of moral enthusiasm extremely low.*

What makes this condition especially significant is that Americans are not naturally an unenthusiastic people. Indeed they have a worldwide reputation for being just the opposite. Visitors to our shores from other countries never cease to marvel at the vigor and energy with which we attack our problems. We live at a fever pitch, and whether we are erecting buildings, laying highways, promoting athletic events, celebrating special days or welcoming returning heroes we always do it with an exaggerated flourish. Our building will be taller, our highway broader, our athletic contest more colorful, our celebration more elaborate and more expensive than would be true anywhere else on earth. We walk faster, drive faster, earn more, spend more and run a higher blood pressure than almost any other people in the world.

In only one field of human interest are we slow and apathetic; that is the field of personal religion. There for some strange reason our enthusiasm flags. Church people habitually approach the matter of their personal relation to God in a dull, halfhearted way which is altogether out of keeping with their general temperament and wholly inconsistent with the importance of the subject.

It is true that there is a lot of religious activity among us. Interchurch basketball tournaments, religious splash parties followed by devotions, weekend camping trips with a Bible quiz around the fire, Sunday school picnics, building fund drives and ministerial breakfasts are with us in unbelievable numbers, and they are carried on with typical American gusto. It is when we enter the sacred precincts of the heart's personal religion that we suddenly lose all enthusiasm.

So we find this strange and contradictory situation: a world of noisy, headlong religious activity carried on without moral energy or spiritual fervor. In a year's travel among the churches one scarcely finds a believer whose blood count is normal and whose temperature is up to standard. The flush and excitement of the soul in love must be sought in the New Testament or in the biographies of the saints; we look for them in vain among the professed followers of Christ in our day.

Now if there is any reality within the whole sphere of human experience that is by its very nature worthy to challenge the mind, engross and charm the heart and bring the total life to a burning focus it is the reality that revolves and shines around the person of Christ. If He is who and what the Christian message declares Him to be, then the thought of Him should be the most exciting, the most stimulating, to enter the human mind. It is not hard to understand how Paul could join wine and the Spirit in one verse, "And be not drunk with wine, wherein is excess; but be filled with the Spirit" (Ephesians 5:18). When the Spirit presents Christ to our inner vision it has an exhilarating effect on the soul much as wine has on the body. The Spirit-filled man may literally dwell in a state of spiritual vivacity amounting to a mild and pure inebriation.

God dwells in a state of perpetual enthusiasm. He is delighted with all that is good and lovingly concerned about all that is wrong. He pursues His labors always in a fullness of holy zeal. No wonder the Spirit came at Pentecost as the sound of a rushing, mighty wind and sat in tongues of fire on every forehead. In so doing He was acting in character with His position as one of the Persons of the blessed Godhead.

Whatever else happened at Pentecost, one thing that cannot be missed by the most casual observer was the sudden upsurging of moral enthusiasm. Those first disciples burned with a steady inward fire. They were enthusiastic to the point of complete abandon.

Dante, on his imaginary journey through hell, came upon a group of lost souls who sighed and moaned continually as they whirled about aimlessly in the dusky air. Virgil, his guide, explained that these were the "wretched people," the "nearly soulless," who while they lived on earth had not moral energy enough to be either good or evil. They had earned neither praise nor blame. And with them and sharing in their punishment were those angels who would take sides neither with God nor Satan. The doom of all of the weak and irresolute crew was to be suspended forever between a hell that despised them and a heaven that would not receive their defiled presence. Not even their names were to be mentioned again in heaven or earth or hell. "Look," said the guide, "and pass on."

Was Dante saying in his own way what our Lord had said long before to the church of Laodicea, "I know thy works, that thou art neither cold nor hot: I would thou wert cold or hot. So then, because thou art lukewarm, and neither cold nor hot, I will spue thee out of my mouth" (Revelation 3:15-16).

The low level of moral enthusiasm among us may have a significance far deeper than we are willing to believe.

Our Low Level of Moral Enthusiasm: Part II

One marked characteristic of present-day Christians is the low level of their spiritual energy, their all but total lack of moral enthusiasm. I do not believe that it is necessary to prove this. We carry the proof in our own hearts and observe it in the conduct of our Christian friends. We may safely accept it as a fact and go on from there.

Back of this condition I believe there are four principal causes. They are:

1. A deadened sense of sin in the Church. The very word *sin* is not in good standing in present-day philosophy and psychology. The intellectuals have put us on the defensive and have made us ashamed to believe in sin as a reality. It is somewhat like believing in nymphs or kelpies, quite all right

for a less educated generation but surely not in keeping with our advanced scientific knowledge. The relativity of morals has been taught to our college youth for a long enough period to give the idea time to sift down into the mind of the man on the street and affect the whole popular concept of right and wrong. Hence there is no sharp line drawn between good and evil, even among church people.

2. The result is that when people "accept" Christ they do so with little or no real conviction for sin and without radical repentance. It is rare now to see a transforming conversion. The average convert becomes one by a series of compromises, whereby he surrenders something to gain something and dickers for his salvation like a huckster. The thought of unconditional surrender to the Lordship of Jesus never enters his mind. A shoddy mercantile theology has reduced the whole thing to the level of an across-the-counter transaction with no loss of face to the sinner. Of course the resultant conversion is a cold-blooded, emotionless affair.

3. Next in order and flowing directly out of these is the absence of an experiential encounter with the living God. The personal encounter gave fire and life to the religion of the Bible. "Abram fell on his face: and God talked with him" (Genesis 17:3). Jacob met God on two occasions and those meetings affected him as light affects a sensitized plate. Moses trembled before God in delighted fear. The Bible itself grew out of such experiences. They were not alike except in their spiritual content and their clear and lasting effect upon the in-

dividual heart. This content is so weak among Christians today as to be all but unrecognizable. The significant words of prophet and apostle were "I saw . . . I heard . . . the heavens were opened . . . I saw the Lord," and other like expressions. Today we try to substitute a pale, waxy "faith" for such vivid encounters. No wonder the Church has taken on the general tone of a convalescent hospital instead of the camp of a victorious army.

4. The fourth cause of our lack of moral enthusiasm, as I see it, is the absence from our experience of an object for the heart's devotion. The great spiritual souls of other days had such an object. In the Old Testament they were frankly and unashamedly in love with the Most High God, and when He became flesh and dwelt among us He came still nearer to the hearts of His people. Paul's heart exploded into a burning volcano of love for the Lord Jesus. It was this and not his theology alone that made him the fiery spirit he was. This it was that gave us Augustine, Bernard, Francis, Rolle, Rutherford and the rest of the shining company.

Today we find ourselves on the fourth step of the chilly stairs that lead downward: 1. No conviction for sin. 2. No transforming conversion. 3. No encounter with God. 4. No object of worship. Where do we go from here?

God Loves Us in His Son

For those who think beneath the surface of things there are some real problems associated with the doctrine of the love of God. What is by many so airily taken for granted because it has been so often repeated is found to hold some positive difficulties when it is examined by the thoughtful and serious-minded Christian.

The first difficulty is one that is likely to bother the soul that is deeply convinced of its own grave sinfulness and its complete unworthiness before God. The problem simply stated is, "How can God love anyone as sinful and worthless as I am?" This question occurs in many of our hymns and is heard in countless prayers and testimonies wherever a group of humble believers come together.

It is not likely that the question will ever be answered to the satisfaction of the penitent heart, for whatever theology says it will always feel its own deep sinfulness and will side against itself and acknowledge that God would be just were He to forsake it forever. Because this is an impulse of the heart and springs not out of reason but out of moral repugnance, there is not much that reason can do to correct it. And I wonder if, after all, we want to eliminate this emotion from the heart entirely. Self-loathing may be carried too far, but a little of it keeps us down where we belong. I think the great saints have always felt it to some degree.

The second problem is a more serious one. It is this: How can a holy God love unholy men? This should not be dismissed lightly, for it involves a real theological predicament. God loves and must love what is like Himself. Now since He is by nature perfectly holy how can He love that which is by nature completely unholy? Man being deceitful above all things and desperately wicked, with every imagination of the thoughts of his heart only evil continually, how can that God who is exactly the opposite of all this find in the sinner anything to love? Would not God's love for that which is radically unlike Himself constitute a moral contradiction and put Him in the position of compromising His holiness?

Of course this is no problem to the quasi-religious person who thinks of God as a great "All-Father" or as merely a kindly spirit that pervades the world, without holiness, justice or truth. A weak, sniveling god who is too loving to condemn sin would have no trouble loving sinners. He could not compromise his holiness for the simple reason that he does not possess any. Such a god is the darling of the starry-eyed religious poet whose creed is love, but he is most surely not the God of the Bible. He is a figment of a fallen and darkened imagination and is as certainly false as were the gods of the Philistines.

To the question, "How can a holy God love an unholy sinner?" there is a full and satisfactory answer. The answer, of course, is found in the teachings of the Scripture. It has been stated for us by the German theologian Eckhart: "The Father loves nothing at all but the Son and such things as He finds in the Son." This is a fair summation of the doctrine of the love of God as presented on the pages of Holy Writ.

"The Father loves nothing at all but the Son." All the love of God is gathered up in Christ. The Father loves the Son with all the love there is, which is to say with all of Himself, and He loves *directly* nothing but the Son. In the Son and through the Son all things came into being, including man. God loves men not for themselves but for the sake of the Son. His love for them is reflected from the face of Jesus Christ and falls upon them only as they are related to the Son. Man was made in God's image and Christ is said to be "the image of the invisible God."

In some mysterious way is the race of mankind related to the Son, and for His sake God can lavish His love upon sinful men and still be just and holy in doing so.

A marginal problem, of no practical importance, is whether or not God continues to love sinners after they have forfeited their rights under the patient forbearance of God and have been consigned to their final place in hell. To believe that He does would be to conceive of Him as being eternally frustrated. Were He to continue forever to pour upon lost men an unrequited love, He could never be at rest. His wasted love would torture Him without end forever.

The truth is that God loves only the Son "and such things as He finds in the Son." When impenitent men have made their final decision against the Son and have walked out of His light for good they will no longer be objects of the love of God. God's love is, like Himself, unchanging and eternal, but it touches only those who touch the Son. The soul that rejects the Son by a final irrevocable act forfeits forever the love of the Father.

Personal Holiness Is First

A selfish desire for happiness is as sinful as any other selfish desire. Its root is in the flesh which can never have any standing before God. "Because the carnal mind is enmity against God: for it is not subject to the law of God, neither indeed can be" (Romans 8:7).

People are coming more and more to excuse every sort of wrongdoing on the grounds that they are "just trying to secure a little happiness." Before she will give her consent to marriage the modern young lady may ask outright whether or not the man "can make me happy." The lovelorn columns of the newspapers are wet with the self-pitying tears of persons who write to inquire how they can "preserve their happiness." The psychiatrists of the land are getting fat off the increasing numbers who seek professional aid in their all-absorbing search for happiness. It is not uncommon for crimes to be committed against persons who do nothing worse than "jeopardize" someone's happiness. This is the hedonistic philosophy of old Grecian days misunderstood and applied to everyday living in the twentieth century. It destroys all nobility of character and makes milksops of all who consciously or unconsciously adopt it; but is quite the popular creed of the masses. That we are born to be happy is scarcely questioned by anyone. No one bothers to prove that fallen men have any moral right to happiness, or that they are in the long run any better off happy. The only question before the house is how to get the most happiness out of life. The thesis of almost all popular books and plays is that personal happiness is the legitimate end of the dramatic human struggle.

Now, I submit that the whole hectic scramble after happiness is an evil as certainly as is the scramble after money or fame or success. It springs out of a vast misunderstanding of ourselves and of our true moral condition. No one who really knows himself can ever believe in his right to be happy. A little glimpse of his own heart will disillusion him instantly so that he is more likely to turn on himself and own God's sentence against him to be just. The doctrine of man's inalienable right to happiness is anti-God and anti-Christ, and its wide acceptance by society tells us a lot about that same society.

The effect of this modern hedonism is felt also among the people of God. The gospel is too often presented as a means toward happiness, to peace of mind or security. There are even those who use the Bible to "relax them," as if it were a drug.

How far wrong all this is will be discovered easily by the simple act of reading the New Testament through once with meditation. There the emphasis is not upon happiness but upon holiness. God is more concerned with the state of people's hearts than with the state of their feelings. Undoubtedly the will of God brings much final happiness to those who obey, but the most important matter is not how happy we are but how holy. The soldier does not seek to be happy; he seeks rather to get the fighting over with, to win the war and get back home to his loved ones. There he may enjoy himself to the full; but while the war is on his most pressing job is to be a good soldier, to acquit himself like a man, regardless of how he feels.

The childish clamor after happiness can become a real snare. One may easily deceive himself by cultivating a religious joy without a correspondingly righteous life. No man should desire to be happy who is not at the same time holy. He should spend his efforts in seeking to know and do the will of God, leaving to Christ the matter of how happy he shall be.

For those who take this whole thing seriously I have a suggestion. Go to God and have an understanding. Tell Him that it is your desire to be holy at any cost and then ask Him never to give you more happiness than holiness. When your holiness becomes tarnished, let your joy become dim. And ask Him to make you holy whether you are happy or not. Be assured that in the end you will be as happy as you are holy; but for the time being let your whole ambition be to serve God and be Christlike. If we are to take a stand like that we may expect to know a new degree of inward purification and, God being who He is, we are more than likely to know a new degree of happiness as well, but a happiness that springs out of a more intimate fellowship with God, a happiness that is elevated and unselfish and free from the carnal drawings of the flesh.

CHAPTER

11

Let's Not Take It for Granted

A little Sunday school song popular a few years ago exhorted us in moments of discouragement to count our many blessings, and it assured us that if we did so we would be astonished at the many things the Lord had done for us.

The song itself is hardly a classic, but it does contain more than a little practical wisdom. We are by nature inclined to be ungrateful and to take as a matter of course the countless blessings God every day showers upon us. We need to keep our thankfulness alive by reminding ourselves how many benefits we enjoy, both as individuals and as a nation.

First, we should be thankful for the Church. With all its faults, the Church has kept the torch of truth burning so that today no one in the civilized world need be in darkness. No one who reads these words but can have abundance of spiritual light if he is interested enough to seek it. Even in these days of declension there are still enough gospel churches to illuminate the public mind. Spiritual darkness where it occurs is the result of indifference. There is plenty of light. The Spirit in the Church has seen to that. And for this we should be deeply grateful.

Then we should be thankful for our country. There is real danger that the doings of cheap politicians should sour us against our own land. Charges and countercharges are being hurled back and forth till the air is blue with them. We must guard against becoming cynical and losing faith in America. Without approving everything we see, there is still sound reason to thank God for our country and all it stands for.

Among the treasures enjoyed by all of us is freedom. Though greatly maligned by its foes and deeply wounded in the house of its friends, it is yet the sweetest thing under the sun next to the Christian religion. Only those who have lost it can fully appreciate it. We are so used to being free that we are in danger of taking our freedom for granted. Let us never do so. We are free at the cost of blood. Many thousands of brave men, who loved life as dearly as we, lie sleeping row on row on a hundred battlefields. They secured for us the right to walk in the sun and to breathe the sweet air of heaven. We should never think of them without bowing our heads in respect to them and in gratitude to God.

For our family also we should each one be thankful. Usually we live too close to our own people to appreciate them as we should. Only after they have left us do we discover how much we owe them. The home is our nursery, our first school, our refuge from life's rough winds and our resting place after the toils of the day. Allowing for its inevitable imperfections, the family and the home are dear beyond words. Father, mother, sister, brother how much we owe them and how little we repay. Thanksgiving should remind us that our own people mean more than we, in our busy preoccupation, are likely to remember.

To our friends and neighbors also we owe a big debt of gratitude. The most "friendless" man, if he will but stop a moment, is likely to discover how many friends he really has after all. Only the man who has like a rogue elephant turned against the herd and put himself outside the bounds of human tolerance may be said to be wholly friendless. And even he may be treated with the most unexpected kindness by policemen, judges and jailers. If the members of society are forced to turn their backs upon the outlaw they seldom do it with bitterness. For the most vicious criminal there remains yet a tattered remnant of love and sympathy.

If this is true of the morally abandoned how much more may the average decent citizen expect and receive understanding and affection. The newspapers know from long experience that a picture of an orphaned baby will bring a hundred inquiries from sympathetic parents who want to adopt it. The story of a needy family will bring in a truckload of gifts from the readers.

And for us Christians, how much closer and dearer are our friendships. They begin here on earth and continue beyond death and enter the world above. For our Christian friends we should be tenderly thankful, and more so as the years go on. We should never take them for granted. They are much too precious for that.

Lastly, because most precious of all, is the friendship and communion of Jesus. He is the friend that sticketh closer than a brother and He has assured us that He will never leave us nor forsake us. Let this knowledge keep us ever thankful. We dare not take Jesus for granted. His love alone should keep the flame of our gratitude at white heat until that day when we shall be presented to the Father with exceeding joy.

There Are Two Sides to the Christian Life

The old devotional writers used to say that there are two kinds of Christian life, the active and the contemplative. And their favorite illustration was the story of Mary and Martha.

Martha stood for the active life, and Mary for the contemplative. The first was concerned with practical service and the second with worship. Of course the contemplative life as represented by Mary was preferred over the other. Martha came to stand for a shallow if useful type of Christian life and the emphasis was placed upon the superiority of the life of prayer and meditation as Mary lived it. Naturally she, not Martha, was held up for emulation.

Now the truth is that Christians cannot be divided into two types and no more, as if Martha does nothing but cook and Mary sits always at Jesus' feet. Human beings are not as simple as that. The most heavenly person must break off meditation sometimes to attend to pressing earthly needs, and the most active Christian must retire sometimes to recharge his spiritual batteries. We are not forced to accept the familiar either/or, to choose to be either a praying Christian or a working one, as if it were not possible to be both. Actually every true Christian *is* both to some degree. The problem is one of balance.

The anonymous author of the celebrated *Cloud of Unknowing*, though very emphatically on the side of the detached, worshiping life, nevertheless admits that the two aspects of the Christian life may be fused into one. "There be," he writes,

two manner of lives in Holy Church. The one is active life, the other is contemplative life. Active is the lower, and contemplative is the higher. Active life hath two degrees, a higher and a lower: and also contemplative life hath two degrees, a lower and a higher. Also these two lives be so coupled together that although they be diverse in some part, yet neither of them may be fully without some part of the other. For why? That part that is the higher part of active life, that same part is the lower part of contemplative life. So that a man may not be fully active, but if he be in part contemplative; nor yet fully contemplative . . . if he be not in part active.

Stated in modern terms this means simply that every real Christian, however practical, is in some degree a mystic, his mysticism lying on the upper side of his life. He prays, meditates on spiritual things and communes with God and the invisible world. Also, every Christian, however he may be dedicated to the holy art of prayer and worship, must of necessity descend to work and eat and sleep and pay his taxes and get on somehow with the hard world around him. And if he follows on to know the Lord he must serve in every useful way outlined for him in the Scriptures of truth. To be a Christian it is necessary that he serve his generation as well as his God.

The big problem is to keep the two elements of the Christian life in proper balance. Math and Mary are sisters and we need both. During the years since Pentecost one and then another of the two has had her day to the exclusion of the other. The pendulum has swung from the practical to the mystical and back again with the passing of the years, and while both sides of the religious life were always present, one side or the other usually got all the attention at a given time. Too bad that even religion must be influenced by intellectual and spiritual fashions.

Today the Christian emphasis falls heavily on the "active" life. People are more concerned with earth than with heaven; they would rather "do something" than to commune with God. The average Christian feels a lot nearer to this world than to the world above. The current vogue favors "Christian action." The favorite brand of Christianity is that sparked by the man in a hurry, hard hitting, aggressive and ready with the neat quip. We are neglecting the top side of our souls. The light in the tower burns dimly while we hurry about the grounds below, making a great racket and giving the impression of wonderful devotion to our task.

The difficult part of this whole thing is to get people to see what is happening to us. The average Christian has accepted the prevailing spiritual mood as normal and is likely to become indignant with anyone who dares to question its soundness or to suggest that the Christian religion as we experience it today is not in every particular one and the same as the religion of the apostles.

It is time that we prayerfully test the flavor of present Christianity and compare its spiritual quality with that of the New Testament. I think we shall find the element of mystic worship all but absent from it. I say all but absent, for it can never be wholly absent. Wherever the Spirit of Christ is present, however imperfectly perceived, the sense of worship will be there in some slight degree.

It is to our lasting reproach that we cannot live full rounded and symmetrical lives, embodying in our redeemed personalities the practical service of Martha and the adoring vision of Mary. We would appear to be unwilling to have both sisters present at once. Just now Martha is all over the premises, but where is Mary? I wish someone would find her soon.

Economic Considerations Kill Religion

D emetrius, the silversmith, could offer no other proof of the truth of his religion than to shout, "Sirs, ye know that by this craft we have our wealth. . . . Great is Diana of the Ephesians!" (Acts 19:25, 28). He encouraged Diana-worship for economic reasons.

An economic interest in religion is deadly. As soon as a man becomes thus entangled in the snare of economic interest he is a true prophet no longer, but a son of mammon. His heart degenerates and his spirit begins to die. Let him perform a religious duty, do a moral act, advocate a reform, or preach a doctrine because he must do so to guarantee his income, and he is no true shepherd now, but a hireling.

That the Church should support its ministers as a country supports its soldiers to free them for the battle is taken for granted by almost all Christians. This arrangement is found in the Old Testament and is carried over into the Church with little change. It is a wise and sound procedure and is above reproach so long as both priest and people are true children of God.

A grave obligation lies upon the church to keep the minister financially free to teach what he from the heart believes. The economic boycott is a weapon sometimes used against the man who insists upon preaching unwelcome truth, and pity the man who is caught in it. Pity more, however, the church that would stoop to exercise it.

Paul had a trade upon which he could fall back when and if the need arose, and I am not sure but it would be a good idea for every preacher to keep a needle and thread handy in case of emergency. Anything is better than to do obeisance to mammon.

A few preachers have found a happy solution to the economic problem in the simple plan of living by faith. No one can put the economic squeeze on such a man; for as he is accountable to God alone for his ministry, God is, by the same token, responsible for his daily bread. It is impossible to starve a man into submission under this arrangement, for the servant of God lives on manna, and manna can be found wherever faith can see it.

Prayer Changes
People—and Things

N o one who has read the Bible with any perception can fail to see that to God men are
more important than things. A human being is of
more value than a thousand galaxies of stars or a
million worlds like ours. God made man in His own
image and He made *things* to serve man. His concern is with intelligent moral beings, not with life-
less matter.

However, since man has a material body and
must live out his days in an environment of matter, time and space, *things* are important to him.
His earthly life is to a large degree interwoven
with matter and the laws that control matter. He
is often deeply affected by the report his senses
bring him from the world around him. Situations

sometimes develop where the welfare of the inner man is for the time allowed to depend somewhat upon outward circumstances. At such times
it is altogether proper that he should pray to God
to alter those circumstances and "change things"
to afford a more favorable climate for the growth
of the spirit. A thousand promises are recorded in
the Scriptures to encourage him to ask and seek
and knock to the end that unfavorable things
might be changed or removed altogether. And
the history of Israel and the Church abundantly
demonstrates that God does hear and answer
prayer.

In all our praying, however, it is important that
we keep in mind that God will not alter His eternal purposes at the word of a man. We do not
pray in order to persuade God to change His
mind. Prayer is not an assault upon the reluctance
of God, nor an effort to secure a suspension of His
will for us or for those for whom we pray. Prayer
is not intended to overcome God and "move His
arm." God will never be other than Himself, no
matter how many people pray, nor how long nor
how earnestly.

God's love desires the best for all of us, and He
desires to give us the best at any cost. He will open
rivers in desert places, still turbulent waves, quiet
the wind, bring water from the rock, send an angel to release an apostle from prison, feed an or-
phanage, open a land long closed to the gospel.
All these things and a thousand others He has
done and will do in answer to prayer, but only be-

cause it had been His will to do it from the beginning. No one persuades Him.

What the praying man does is to bring His will into line with the will of God so God can do what He has all along been willing to do. Thus prayer changes the man and enables God to change things in answer to man's prayer.

Three Factors That Make a Deed Good

Every Christian wants to do good. He knows that he is not saved by his good deeds, but he knows also that good deeds will follow his salvation and be the practical proof that it is real. And he knows that he will someday stand before the judgment seat of Christ to receive the consequences of deeds done in the body, whether they be good or evil.

To be good a deed must pass three tests: What? Why? and How? What we do is, of course, important. There are deeds that are wrong in themselves; nothing can make them right and no circumstances can excuse them. Such we will pass by for the moment and give our attention to those acts that are considered good without question by the generality of mankind.

At the risk of being thought repetitious I'll say again that in religion and morals motive comes very near to being everything. It is not *what* a man does only but *why* he does it that determines the moral quality of the deed. A deed which on the surface may be good, if done for a selfish reason is actually evil. And since we cannot often penetrate to the springs of human conduct we cannot always be sure whether the deeds of others are good or bad. Charity dictates that we give every man the advantage of the doubt, but God alone knows the facts. I trust that most of us serve God and our fellow men from motives that will stand the test of Why?

But there is another factor about which I find it impossible to be wholly optimistic. It is *how* our good deeds are done; that is, the spirit in which we do them. I think it is possible to pass the first two tests and fail the third dismally.

Above all persons the Christian should be gracious and self-effacing. His alms should be given in private and as unostentatiously as possible. He should avoid making the recipient feel embarrassed. A loan may be made, for instance, in such a manner that the one who receives it may be humiliated and hurt so deeply that the later repayment of the loan will not square the transaction. He will feel cheap and inferior for a long time simply because the loan was made in a wrong spirit.

A little poem says in few words what I have in mind:

Inglorious
And a shame to see,

Is a favor done
Ungraciously.

I am afraid there are a great many favors done
so ungraciously as to be no favors at all but actual
injuries to the persons receiving them. Most of us
at some time have had the painful experience of
being made to feel small by a favor done with a
superior air or a tolerant smile. We Christians
should study and pray for the grace of casualness
when helping a friend. I have known a few persons who have been able to do a favor in such a
way as to create the feeling that they themselves
were being favored. Such an art is as rare as it is
beautiful. We should cultivate it more carefully.

It is scarcely necessary to point out that a contribution made grudgingly will not be accepted by
the Lord. A sour gift is no gift at all even if it is
given to the poor or to foreign missions. Religious
work done under protest might as well be left un-
done. It is not good in fact, however excellent it
may seem to be.

The sum of the matter is that our works, to be
good, must have our hearts in them. They must
be the works of the Spirit, done in the Spirit. Short
of this they are but wood, hay and stubble.

No Christian Should Feel Contempt

One of the hardest sayings in the New Testament is this: "Whosoever shall say to his brother, Raca, shall be in danger of the council: but whosoever shall say, Thou fool, shall be in danger of hell fire" (Matthew 5:22).

What our Lord is saying here is not that a man will be punished with hell fire for calling another a fool, but that a man who can say "Thou fool" to a fellow man is revealing a state of heart which will fit him for hell in the end. Not the relatively slight offense of calling a brother a fool, but the serious sin of *contempt* endangers a man's future. The gravity of the situation lies not in the fact that a man can cry "Fool!" but that he can feel the contempt which the word expresses.

Contempt for a human being is an affront to God almost as grave as idolatry, for while idolatry is disrespect for God Himself, contempt is disrespect for the being He made in His own image. Contempt says of a man, "*Raca!* This fellow is of no worth. I attach to his person no value whatsoever." The man guilty of thus appraising a human being is thoroughly bad; and for a number of reasons.

Contempt is an emotion possible only where there is great pride. The error in moral judgment that undervalues another always springs out of the error that overvalues oneself. The contemptuous man esteems himself too highly for reasons that are invalid. His high opinion of himself is not based upon his position as a being made in God's image; he esteems himself for fancied virtues which he does not possess. He is wrong in his attitude toward himself and doubly wrong in his estimation of his fellow man. The error in his judgment is moral, not intellectual.

It is in the realm of religion that contempt finds its most fruitful soil and flourishes most luxuriantly. It is seen in the cold disdain with which the respectable church woman regards the worldly sister and in the scorn heaped upon the fallen woman by the legally married wife. The sober deacon may find it hard to conceal his contempt for the neighbor who drinks. The evangelical may castigate the liberal in a manner that leaves slight doubt that he feels himself above him in every way. Religion that is not purified by penitence, humility and love, will lead to a feeling of contempt for the irreligious and the morally degraded. And since contempt implies a judgment of no worth made against a human brother, the contemptuous man comes under the displeasure of God and proves himself to lie in danger of hell fire.

The Christian cannot close his eyes to good and evil in his fellow men. He cannot avoid rendering moral judgment on the deeds of men; and, indeed, he is accountable to do so. "Ye shall know them by their fruits" (Matthew 7:16). "From such turn away" (2 Timothy 3:5). But his disapprobation of the evil ways of men must not betray him into contempt for their humanity. He must reverence the humanity of every man, however degraded, out of appreciation for his divine origin. No one for whom Christ died can be common or worthless. Humanity itself must be honored as the garment assumed by the Eternal Son in the Incarnation. To esteem anyone worthless who wears the form of a man is to be guilty of an affront to the Son of Man. We should hate sin in ourselves and in all men, but we should never undervalue the man in whom the sin is found.

We Must Be
Church-Minded

S o precious is the Church in the eyes of God
that it is scarcely possible it should ever become too precious in the eyes of men. "I love Thy
Church, O God," should be next after "I love Thee,
O Lord."

The Church is the temple in which the Spirit of
Christ dwells, the body of which Christ is the
Head, the medium through which He works for
the reclamation of mankind. Individual members
of the Church working in harmony with each
other are the lips and hands and feet of the
inliving Christ. The Church is the true Shekinah,
the visible habitation of the invisible God, the
Bride of Christ, destined to share forever the love
of His heart and the privileges of His throne.

It is, of course, not possible at this time to have the whole together again "all with one accord in one place" (Acts 2:1). Some of her members have gone to join the Church of the Firstborn in heaven and now mingle with the spirits of just men made perfect. And they who still remain on earth form a company too vast ever to assemble in one building. The gathering of the whole Church in one place must wait the consummation. Only the city four-square will provide sufficient room for such a joyous assembly.

While the whole Church cannot come together on earth, God has ordered it so that the same thing can be realized on a limited scale by the gathering together of small groups of believers in the fellowship of worship and prayer. Any assembly of true Christians is a church. "For where two or three are gathered together in my name, there am I in the midst of them" (Matthew 18:20). The name and the Presence are indispensable to a local church. A group of saved persons, however small, who meet in Christ's name and recognize His Presence, form a true cell in His body and enjoy the full power and authority of Christ Himself.

Because this is true the whole Christian psychology should be tuned to Christ and the Church. Every worshiper should keep before him the thought of Christ and His Church. However humble the external circumstances, if Christ is present the place is a holy temple and every believer a priest before the altar. Each single cell is an organic part of the larger body and is joined to the whole and to the Lord who indwells it by the life of the inliving Spirit.

A sense of the unity of the Church should dictate our attitude toward it and shape the polity of the local assembly. Constant emphasis should be laid upon the fact that the local church is one indivisible organization and that there can be no independent "brotherhood" or "youth church" or "children's church" operating apart from the life and order of the whole. Departments within the church may seem to be necessary and may actually make for smoother functioning, especially where the church is a large one; but when any department begins to think of itself as a thing apart, unrelated to the local body, it becomes a cancer on the church's life and leads to its final destruction.

A multitude of religious organizations has grown up in recent times, most of them dedicated to one specific spiritual task. Among these we may list Bible societies, Bible schools and various business and professional groups bearing the name Christian. Undoubtedly many of these are good and useful agents through which the Church may work, but they must never be allowed to substitute for the Church. They are handmaids only; they can never take the place of the true mistress.

When all has been said, it is still true that the most perfect expression of God's will on earth will be found in the local church, whose members meet at stated times and places to worship the Lord and commune with each other and then go out to serve their generation after the manner laid down in the Scriptures.

CHAPTER

18

We Need Deliverance
from Carnal Fear

fear of man's judgement

C arnal fear may take either of two opposite directions. It may make us afraid to do what we know we should do, or afraid not to do what we have reason to think people expect us to do. Courage lies somewhere between these two extremes.

There is a foolish consistency which brings us into bondage to the consciences of other people. Our Christian testimony has created a certain expectation in the minds of our friends, and rather than jeopardize our standing with them we dutifully act in accordance with their expectation even though we have no inward conviction on the matter. We are simply afraid not to do what people expect of us. We cannot face our public after we have failed to do what we know they expected us to do.

This morality by public pressure is not pure morality at all. At best it is a timid righteousness of doubtful parentage; at worst it is the child of weakness and fear. A free Christian should act from within with a total disregard for the opinions of others. If a course is right he should take it because it is right, not because he is afraid not to take it. And if it is wrong he should avoid it, though he lose every friend, his property, his freedom and even his very life as a consequence.

Fear of the opinion of the group tends to regiment the members of denominations and churches and force them into a cooky-cutter uniformity. The desire to stand well with our own circle of religious friends destroys originality and makes imitators out of us. Various churches have their approved experiences, their shibboleths, even their accepted religious tones; these become standard for the group and are to the local fellowship what circumcision was to Israel, a ceremonial token of acceptance into the clan.

The great fault in all this is that it shifts the life motivation from within to without, from God to our fellow man. Any act done because we are afraid not to do it must take its place along with any act that is not done because we are afraid to do it. Fear, not love and faith, dictates the conduct, and whatsoever is not of faith is sin.

The way to escape this double snare is simple. Make a complete surrender to God; love Him with all your heart and love every man for His sake. Determine to obey your own convictions as they crystallize within you as a result of prayer and constant study of the Scriptures. After that you may safely ignore the expectations of your friends as well as the criticisms of your enemies. You will experience first the shocked surprise of the regimented army of lock-step believers, then their grudging admiration, and if you continue to walk the way of love and courage they will take heart from your example, throw off the bondage of fear and go forth as ransomed men and women to walk in the sweet liberty wherewith Christ has made them free.

[handwritten marginal notes: "surrender to God; love Him & all others for His sake, not theirs. ⓐ pray ⓑ study Scripture"]

[handwritten notes at bottom: "shibboleth: any custom or tradition particularly a speech pattern that distinguishes one group of people (in group) from others (out group)"]

CHAPTER

19

We Must Not
Be Afraid to Look

In reading such men as Wesley and Finney one is struck with the bold way they dealt with hindrances to God's work wherever they found them. They dared to look at any work of religion, to examine the claims of any would-be prophet, and appraise them for what they were worth. They were thus able to purge out those false elements which, if allowed to remain, would soon have brought the work of God to a stop.

This is an art which very much needs to be revived in the tricky times in which we live. We now seem afraid to probe into anything that claims to be of God lest we violate the spirit of love or lay irreverent hands upon the ark.

Have we forgotten that we labor under a direct injunction to "try the spirits" (1 John 4:1) and "prove

60

all things" (1 Thessalonians 5:21)? Through our failure to obey this charge a hundred abuses are allowed to linger within the Church, weakening it, hindering it and throwing it open to just reproach.

The fashion now is to tolerate anything lest we gain the reputation of being intolerant. The tenderminded saints cannot bear to see Agag slain (see 1 Samuel 15), so they choose rather to sacrifice the health of the Church for years to come by sparing error and evil; and this they do in the name of Christian love.

We are under obligation to disturb all seats of wickedness, and where this is done out of sincere love for God and men, great good is bound to follow. No true work of God will suffer from the prayerful examination of Spirit-filled men. Timidity masquerading as love has allowed useless forms and unscriptural practices to persist in many a church till they have slowly smothered the life out of it and brought it to desolation. And many a promising work of revival has been wrecked because no one was courageous enough to stand against the abuses that entered to destroy it.

We must not be afraid to inquire. The difficulty, of course, is to do this in a Christian spirit. It is hard to find fault without being a faultfinder or to criticize without being censorious. But we have it to do if we hope to keep the work of God pure in a day of iniquity.

Integration or Repudiation?

The world seems to possess a real genius for being wrong, even the educated world. We might just let that pass and go fishing except that we Christians happen to be living in the world and we have an obligation to be right—in everything, all of the time. We cannot afford to be wrong.

I can see how a right man might live in a wrong world and not be much affected by it except that the world will not let him alone. It wants to educate him. It is forever coming up with some new idea which, by the way, is usually an old idea dusted off and shined up for the occasion, and demanding that everyone, including the said right man, conform on pain of deep-seated frustration or a horrible complex of some kind.

Society, being fluid, usually moves like the wind, going all out in one direction until the novelty wears off or there is a war or a depression. Then the breeze sets another way and everyone is supposed to go along with it without asking too many question, though this constant change of direction should certainly cause the thoughtful soul to wonder whether anyone really knows that all the excitement is about after all.

Right now the zephyrs are blowing in the direction of social integration, sometimes also called social adjustment. According to this notion society is possessed of a norm, a sort of best-of-all-possible model after which we must all pattern ourselves if we want to escape sundry psychosomatic disorders and emotional upsets. The only safety for any of us is in becoming so well adjusted to the other members of society as to reduce the nervous and mental friction to a minimum. Education therefore should first of all teach adjustment to society. Whatever people happen to be interested in at the moment must be accepted as normal, and any nonconformity on the part of anyone is bad for the individual and harmful to everybody. Our highest ambition should be to become integrated to the mass, to lose our moral individuality in the whole.

However absurd this may appear when thus stated baldly it is nevertheless a fair description of the most popular brand of philosophy now engaging the attention of society. So many and so efficient are the media of mass communication that when the Brahmans of the educational world decide that it is time for the wind to change, the commonalty quickly get the drift and swing obediently into the breeze. Anyone who resists is a kill-joy and a spoilsport, to say nothing of being old-fashioned and dogmatic.

Well, if to escape the charge of being dogmatic I must accept the changing dogmas of the masses, then I am willing to be known as a dogmatist and no holds barred. We who call ourselves Christians are supposed to be a people apart. We claim to have repudiated the wisdom of this world and adopted the wisdom of the cross as the guide of our lives. We have thrown in our lot with that One who while He lived on earth was the most unadjusted of the sons of men. He would not be integrated into society. He stood above it and condemned it by withdrawing from it even while dying for it. Die for it He would, but surrender to it He would not.

The wisdom of the cross is repudiation of the world's "norm." Christ, not society, becomes the pattern of the Christian life. The believer seeks adjustment, not to the world, but to the will of God, and just to the degree that he is integrated into the heart of Christ is he out of adjustment with fallen human society. The Christian sees the world as a sinking ship from which he escapes not by integration but by abandonment.

A new moral power will flow back into the Church when we stop preaching social adjustment and begin to preach social repudiation and cross carrying. Modern Christians hope to save the world by being like it, but it will never work. The Church's power over the world springs out of her unlikeness to it, never from her integration into it.

CHAPTER

21

On Provocation

The word provoke means to stir up, to arouse. It may be used in a good sense but is so used only rarely. Mostly it refers to the act of making people angry by some real or supposed affront.

We have all noticed how quick many people are to excuse themselves for some outburst by pleading that they were provoked to it. Thus their own wrongdoing is laid to others. What is overlooked in this neat trick of self-exoneration is that provocation cannot stir up what is not there. It never adds anything to the human heart; it merely brings out what is already present. It does not change the character; it simply reveals it.

What a man does under provocation is what he is. The mud must be at the bottom of the pool or it cannot be stirred up. You cannot roil pure water.

Provocation does not create the moral muck; it brings it to the surface. No more.

A holy man cannot be provoked to unholy acts. A pure-hearted man may be stirred to action by any of several stimuli, but the action will always accord with the purity of his heart. "[Charity] is not easily provoked," said Paul in First Corinthians 13:5, and the word "easily" is generally held to be an interpolation. "Charity is not provoked," say the majority of translations, though some put the word irritated for provoked, making it read, "Charity is not irritable." But granted that love may be provoked, it can never be provoked to any act incompatible with itself. If it is stirred to action the action will be in accord with its own nature. Love can never be anything but love.

It may bring some kind of cheap consolation to the man who has just lost his temper or let himself go in a display of bad disposition to consider that he was provoked to it by the act of another, but if he values his soul he will not thus excuse himself. Honesty will compel him to admit that he had a bad disposition to start with and the provocation merely brought it to the surface. The fault is his own, not that of the one who exposed it.

One thing yet should be added: The New Testament warns that those who incite others to evil acts will themselves be brought to stern justice. The devil tempted Christ but could not persuade Him to do wrong. Christ could not be stirred to evil because there was no evil in Him to stir. Satan's efforts were wasted, and no harm was done;

nevertheless he must yet face the terror of God's judgment for his unholy attempt. Whoever puts a stumbling block in the path of the Christian will receive just punishment whether or not he succeeds in causing him to fall. Before the pool can be muddied the muck must indeed be at the bottom, but the hot anger of God will move against the one who delights to stir it up.

Faith or Imagination

When considering the resurrection of Christ and the promised future resurrection of the redeemed, we may at times be disturbed by a sense of unreality about the whole thing. We just cannot picture it. The thought of it is so completely unlike anything that has occurred in our experience that our minds cannot find a definite place to light; so they flutter over the idea like a bird over unfamiliar terrain.

No doubt this bothers many of God's people not a little. They fear that the mental uncertainty they feel is a proof of unbelief and wonder whether they actually believe in the resurrection of the body as taught in the New Testament and repeated in the Creed. I believe these fears are groundless. Here's why:

These "fearful saints" are confusing two things which are wholly unlike each other, that is, they are confusing faith and imagination. Faith is confidence in the character of a moral being which takes the word of that being as completely trustworthy and rests in it without question. Imagination is the power to visualize, to create in the mind a picture of things unseen. We may have either one without the other. The two are not identical and are indeed only distantly related.

A soldier has been overseas two or three years and is now on his way home. As he gets closer to his native shores anticipation mounts in his heart. He visualizes the joyous meeting soon to take place. He pictures his mother, his sister, his wife, and he smiles as he thinks of how much his little son may have grown since he saw him last. The whole scene is before him as he dreams of the long-awaited reunion. Intelligence dictates a slight difference in the appearance of his loved ones. He knows they will have changed, and he tries to adjust his mental image accordingly. He thus visualizes an event which has not yet occurred by drawing on past experience.

It is right here that thought breaks down when it comes to the resurrection. We have no experience to guide us. When Christ rose from the dead He did what no one had ever done before. We cannot imagine how He accomplished the miracle. We are not even sure exactly what wonderful thing happened there in the silence of Joseph's new tomb. That He came forth, alive forevermore, has been the firmly settled faith of the Church from the beginning. How He accomplished it is a secret locked in the mind of God. We should remember the wise admonition of John Wesley: "Let us not doubt a fact because we do not know how it was accomplished." The resurrection of Christ is a fact. More than that we need not know.

Our own future resurrection is even harder to visualize. To paint a mental picture of our death is not so difficult because it has been our experience that everyone goes out that way.

> Thou knowest 'tis common,—all that live
>   must die,
> Passing through nature to eternity.

The mind can visualize our departure from this earth because it has something to guide it in forming its mental picture, but the resurrection affords it no familiar stuff with which to work. And here is where anxiety and self-reproach enter. Because we cannot visualize it we are afraid that we do not believe it.

The hope of the resurrection is a matter of pure faith. It rests upon the character of God and draws its comfort from the knowledge that God cannot lie nor deceive nor change. He has promised that all who sleep in Jesus shall be brought again from their graves to meet the Lord in the air and be with Him forever. The New Testament is filled with this joyful expectation. How God will bring it all to pass is not for us to know. We are not called to understand, but to believe.

Though a detailed knowledge of the mysterious ways of God in accomplishing the resurrection were possible for us, I wonder if we would be any better off for it. We honor God more by believing Him to do the impossible. And after all, nothing is impossible with God.

Are We Having a Revival of True Religion? Part I

That there has been a large-scale return to religion in the Western world, and more particularly in the United States, is too evident to need much proof. Religion is in vogue again. It is now considered smart to be religious.

This movement toward religion set in about the time of the Second World War and has continued ever since, in violent contrast to the attitudes that prevailed after the First World War. Civilized men came out of that first world struggle bitter, cynical, disillusioned and thoroughly angry with God. False prophets, in and out of the pulpits, had led people to believe that the race had progressed so far in the direction of universal brotherhood that war had become impossible. The arguments they advanced in support of their belief were too fragile to stand up under the battering of facts, but faith in peace and brotherhood had come on the world like a Yo-yo epidemic and everybody that was anybody was playing with it. The only voices that sounded a discordant note in the universal chorus of peace were those of the Fundamentalists who were ignored completely as being unlearned, reactionary and 200 years behind the times. So cheerfully singing a lullaby of "Peace, peace," the world plunged into a blood bath the like of which had not been known or imagined up to that time. What the people did not believe could happen did happen before their eyes. Like Cain of old, the world was exceeding wroth and its countenance fell. God had let the human race down. Religion was a fraud. Piety was hypocrisy and prayer a throwback to the jungle. They would have no more of that.

An embittered world took revenge on the hope that had failed it by debunking everything formerly considered sacred. The popular writers of the period gleefully exposed the weaknesses of everyone in history that had enjoyed a reputation for godliness or even plain decency. The Puritans were shown to be hard, cruel men who hated the human race; the Pilgrim Fathers were tried and found guilty of downright hypocrisy. Washington was a whisky sot and Lincoln a neurotic who loved off-color stories and used religion only as a convenient cloak. And so it was with everyone and everything else associated with religion.

Hardly anyone of any prominence in literary and philosophical circles believed in God. A "new era" was just ahead when the "new masses" would rise up, throw off the yoke of religion and establish a "new republic," a Marxian utopia having most of the characteristics of the Biblical millennium, but with one important difference: this man-made golden age would have no place for God or Christ or the Bible. Or if there were to be a Bible it would not be the Hebrew-Christian book given by divine inspiration, but a humanistic anthology composed of select passages from writers of the stripe of Lucretius, Rosseau and Shaw, compiled very likely by Henry Mencken or H.G. Wells.

A new dream of peace and brotherhood had come to the world, rising this time not from misplaced religious faith, as the previous dream had done, but from a thoroughly mundane secularism that would have no part of God or religion. The spiritual atmosphere between the two wars was materialistic, skeptical and self-confident. The prevailing ideology was a watered-down and disguised communism. The Commies were romping all over the White House lawn, lecturing in our universities and writing for our best magazines. The prevailing mood was humanistic. The motivating philosophies varied from each other in minor details, but they were all "one world" philosophies. This world was all that mattered. Anything beyond it was speculative and unproved. Faith in a world above was mere wishful thinking and could actually slow down human progress by lulling men into inactivity.

In such a soul state the civilized world moved into the unspeakable horrors of World War II. Then the wholesale murder of civilian populations, the incredible iniquities of the Nazis, the shocking collapse of trust among the nations of the earth, the monstrous violations of the spirit of brotherhood, the inhumanity of man to man, the triumph of perfidy, the near ending of civilization, and finally the appearance of weapons potentially capable of bringing a flaming end to the human race itself—all this quite literally scared people into a return to religion. The humanists had failed. The starry-eyed faith in man's ability to find his way alone was bombed and burned out of people's hearts. The world began to look around for God.

So came about the return to religion. The mid-fifties finds the pendulum swung to the opposite extreme from where it was in the mid-twenties. Religion is back in style again. People can now talk about their faith without apology. It is intellectually respectable again to believe in God. The religious motif is back in the literary and entertainment world once more. Just everybody and anybody is willing to come forward and say, "This I believe." And no one acts embarrassed or changes the subject. Religion is back in fashion.

The fact cannot be disputed.

CHAPTER

24

Are We Having a Revival of True Religion? Part II

Religion is again legal in America. It is no longer necessary to whisper about it behind our hand. It is back in season.

The secular press, which of course is always quick to sense trends and give the public what it wants, has found that religion is news. A sufficiently large number of those who buy newspapers and magazines are interested enough in religion to make it profitable to print increasingly generous amounts of religious copy. Religious books are among the best sellers. Prominent people are telling the world what they believe. Religion is woven into sports, politics, the theatre. It is frequently a part of night club chatter, and the radio and TV comedian has learned that a serious word about prayer and church going at the end of his routine will please most of his listeners. That is not all. The three major religious faiths in the United States are spending huge sums in advertising and are competing for attention in the press and on the radio. So many churches and other religious structures are being built these days that the building industry, which once considered such things something of a dead weight, is pretty well steamed up about the whole thing and is now quite eager to have the religious trade. Church membership is growing out of all proportion to the growth of the population. Converts to one or another religion are being sought on every level of society and among all classes and age groups. We have zealous work going on among children and young people. We are using sound trucks, radio, television, streetcar cards, billboards, neon signs, messages in bottles and on balloons. We are using trained horses, trained dogs, trained canaries, ventriloquists, magicians and drama to stir up religious interest. Innumerable professional guilds, industrial clubs and business men's and women's committees have sprung up to provide spiritual fellowship for religious-minded persons engaged in the various pursuits of life. Religious songs are in the repertoire of many professional entertainers. Religion is being plugged by night club entertainers, prize fighters, movie stars, and by at least one incarcerated gangster who has up to this time shown no sorrow for his way of life and no evidence of repentance. Religion, if you please, is now big business.

Unquestionably much of the religious activity of the day is good and in keeping with the ways of God as revealed in the Scriptures. Conversely, a lot of it is worldly, carnal and wholly indefensible in the light of revealed truth. Everything I have stated here is true and is too well known to be disputed. The facts are before us. The questions that are troubling many serious-minded persons are these: Do these facts add up to a revival of true religion? Is this that? Is what we are growing so luxuriantly wheat or tares? or is it a mixture of both? If it is both, do we see a great field of wheat with a few tares? or a wilderness of tares with an occasional stalk of wheat? Is this new interest in religion a result of the operation of the Holy Spirit? Is this resurgence of religious zeal on a level with that which swept over Germany in the days of Luther, or over England in the time of Wesley? In short, is this New Testament Christianity?

To some people these questions are meaningless, and if they bothered to notice them almost every answer would be "yes." The secular press greets the current return to religion with starry-eyed optimism, and even the religious press either hails it as a triumph for the Kingdom of God or ventures no appraisal at all. I think it may be conservatively stated that the great majority of our religious leaders accept the present swing toward religion as a genuine expression of a deep human longing after God and righteousness and want to encourage it all they can. Though some of them privately deplore many things associated with this religious movement they are too cautious to speak out. Their position is: It may not be perfect but it is better than nothing. So let the good work go on.

My purpose in these six chapters is to appraise the religious phenomenon which I have called (appropriating a phrase from Dr. Link) "a return to religion." Knowing that my words will be about as welcome to many persons as were the words of Micaiah at the court of King Ahab, I yet venture to say that I am not too happy about the way things are going. While I thank God reverently for any shreds of true Christianity that may be left among us, I am far from encouraged by what my eyes behold in the religious world. I'll give my reasons in the remaining four chapters in this series.

Are We Having a Revival of True Religion? Part III

At this point it would appear necessary to define terms. Before communication can be established between writer and reader there must be a common understanding as to the meaning of words. I'll explain what I mean by "true religion."

To the convinced Christian there can be but one true religion. The half-converted may shy away from the bigotry and intolerance which he fears lie in an exclusive devotion to Christianity, but the wholly converted will have no such apprehensions. To him Christ is all in all and the faith of Christ is God's last word to mankind. To him there is but one God, the Father; one Lord and Savior, one faith, one baptism, one body, one Spirit, one fold and one Shepherd. To him there is none other name under heaven given among men whereby we must be saved. For him Christ is the only way, the only truth and the only life. For him Christ is the only wisdom, the only righteousness, the only sanctification and the only redemption. He knows that his convictions will bring him into disrepute with the so-called liberals, and he knows he will be branded as narrow and "seventeenth century" in his thinking. But he is willing to bear the stigma. What he has seen and heard and experienced precludes any possibility of compromise. He must be true to the heavenly vision.

When, therefore, I ask the question, "Are we having a revival of true religion?" I have only one religion in mind. I mean the faith of the New Testament as held and experienced by the Fathers. I mean that religion of which Moses and all the prophets did write, that religion which originated in the heart of God the Father, was made effectual through the hard dying and triumphant resurrection of God the Son and is vitalized and propagated among men by God the Holy Spirit. Of this religion the Hebrew and Christian Scriptures are the source book, the first and last word, to which we dare add nothing and from which we dare take nothing away.

If the reader does not agree with my definition of true religion, then communication between us breaks down. There is no point in using words which mean one thing to me and another to the reader. Unless we agree to let the Scriptures tell us what true religion is, there is no way for us to find out. Each man is thrown back into the depths of his own dark ignorance and must feel his way along the steep sides of the abyss from which there is no escape.

If, on the other hand, we agree to let the Word of God decide what is and is not the religion of Christ, an inspired pattern is established for us and we are saved from tragic and costly errors concerning this all-important matter.

Once this standard is acknowledged it is not too difficult to test a given doctrine or practice to determine whether it is of God or not. We have only to compare everything that professes to be New Testament Christianity with the New Testament itself. "To the law and to the testimony: if they speak not according to this word, it is because there is no light in them" (Isaiah 8:20).

Every activity now being carried on in the name of Christ must meet the last supreme test: Does it have biblical authority back of it? Is it according to the letter and the spirit of the Scripture? Is its spiritual content divinely given? That it succeeds proves nothing. That it is popular proves less. Where are the proofs of its heavenly birth? Where are its scriptural credentials? What assurance does it give that it represents the operation of the Holy Spirit in the divine plan of the ages? These questions demand satisfactory answers.

No one should object to an honest examination of his work in the pure light of Scripture. No honest man will shrink from the light, nor will he defend beliefs and practices that cannot be justified by the test of truth. Rather he will eagerly seek to build according to the pattern shown him in the mount.

> Therefore whosoever heareth these sayings of mine, and doeth them, I will liken him unto a wise man, which built his house upon a rock; And the rain descended, and the floods came, and the winds blew, and beat upon that house; and it fell not: for it was founded upon a rock. (Matthew 7:24-25)

Are we today building on the rock? Upon the answer hangs our little all. We had better be sure.

Are We Having a Revival of True Religion? Part IV

In an attempt to discover whether the present increase in religious interest indicates a genuine revival of biblical Christianity I propose some easy tests. First: *Is the spiritual content of current popular religion identical with or even close to that of the New Testament? Is this that?*

I do not mean to imply that a true religious revival must be free from faults. To require perfection in the work of God among fallen men would not be realistic. Though God is perfect, men are not, and God must deal with them as He finds them. The work of Christ was flawless, but the response of His followers was imperfect and full of faults. The New Testament Epistles and the seven letters of the book of Revelation reveal that the first Christians were not always models of perfection. Every reformation and revival from Pentecost to modern times has had its faults, its vagaries and excesses along with its purity and its power. All this we freely admit. We do not require perfection as a proof of the genuineness of revival.

What we do require before we will admit its authenticity is that the spirit, the temper, of a religious movement must be scriptural. The color and flavor must be that of the New Testament. The spiritual essence of the Gospels and Epistles must appear in any religious phenomenon or it is instantly disqualified and must be rejected as spurious.

By this test it is plain that the current return to religion is not a return to the faith of Christ and the apostles. The temper is not the same; the spiritual content is of another essence; the quality is not only inferior but of another kind altogether. By every spiritual test this is not that.

True, the voice is Jacob's voice. The current return to religion is ostensibly a return to the faith of Christ, for the language employed is that of the Bible. But the hands are the hands of Esau. The practice is not consonant with the testimony. The two are not only different from, they are hostile to, each other.

Except in rare and isolated instances current Christianity is not producing godliness. And where an example of true saintliness appears occasionally it will be found to be a throwback to another and more serious type of religion than that to which people have "returned" in such numbers today. My own observation has taught me that the few who are yearning to be Christlike are being forced to dissent from most of what they see around them and go it alone in their holy longing after God. Scarcely any religious activities today conduce to holiness. The hungry seeker after personal godliness must look beyond the current "revival." He'll not find much help there.

If anyone should wonder what I mean by godliness, saintliness, holiness, I'll explain. I mean a life and a heart marked by *meekness* and *humility*. The godly soul will not boast nor show off. I mean *reverence*. The godly man will never take part in any religious exercise that shows disrespect for the Deity. The cozy, cute terms now applied to God and Christ will never pass his lips. He will never join in singing religious songs that are light, humorous or irreverent. He will cultivate a spirit of complete sincerity and discuss God and religion only in grave and reverent tones.

Further, I mean *separation* from the world unto God in an all-out, irrevocable committal. The holy man will not envy the world, nor will he imitate it or seek its approval. His testimony will be, "I am crucified unto the world and the world unto me." He will not depend upon it for his enjoyments, but will look above and within for the joy that is unspeakable and full of glory.

In short, any true work of God in the churches will result in an intensified spirit of worship and an elevated appreciation of the basic Christian virtues as they are set forth in the New Testament. It will result in self-denial and cross carrying among the people. It will make men Christlike, will free them from a thousand carnal sins they did not even know were sins before. It will free them from earthly entanglements and focus their whole attention upon things above.

This is not a dreamer's view of the Christian faith. The New Testament abundantly supports what is written here. In the light of the facts, may we conclude that the current wave of religious interest is an indication that a revival is on? Obviously not. And there are other and more convincing tests to come.

Are We Having a Revival of True Religion? Part V

Were a resurgence of the true faith of Christ to occur anywhere in the civilized world we would have every right to expect those affected by it to become more spiritual, more saintly, in the best sense of these words. The present wave of religion is having no such effect. Indeed the whole concept of saintliness is absent. The yearning to be holy can scarcely be found among the busy religionists of the day.

Christianity once set out to convert the world and ended by undergoing a reverse conversion. The world converted the Church, and after the passing of sixteen centuries we are still suffering from the disgraceful surrender. Rome introduced her pagan ways into the pure stream of the Christian faith and the waters are still muddy after how many noble efforts to purify them. And that great half-Christian, half-pagan institution, the Roman Catholic Church, which took its rise at the time of that historic reverse conversion, moves on from victory to victory and continues to spread itself across the face of the whole world.

The rise of a new religious spirit in recent years is marked by disturbing similarities to that earlier "revival" under Constantine. Now as then a quasi-Christianity is achieving acceptance by compromise. It is dickering with the unregenerate world for acceptance and, as someone said recently, it is offering Christ at bargain prices to win customers. The total result is a conglomerate religious mess that cannot but make the reverent Christian sick in his heart.

Without the remotest intention to accept the authority of Christ many religious leaders nevertheless use His name as an attractive front to give them entree to the masses. Whether or not it is the fulfillment of that odd passage in Isaiah, still it reminds one of the words, "And in that day seven women shall take hold of one man, saying, We will eat our own bread, and wear our own apparel: only let us be called by thy name, to take away our reproach" (Isaiah 4:1). Doctrines wholly foreign to the Scriptures are being taught in the name of Christ (as, for instance, the strange humanistic hodgepodge of Norman Vincent Peale); and His name is being pronounced over deeds as carnal and earthly as any ever performed under the sun. The "Man Upstairs" of war days is now being invoked to bring success to the selfish schemes of unregenerate men.

One movie star, after a half hour of fighting, shooting and general mayhem closes his radio show with the folksy benediction, "May the good Lord take a likin' to you." A night club gossip monger ends his broadcast with the exhortation, "And go with God." A disc jockey who broadcasts from a saloon has been known to interview religious persons on his program and to draw them out to tell of the power of prayer. A famous night club comedian publicly testifies that he became a thousand-dollar-a-week success after praying to a statue and promising to contribute generously of his income to humanitarian purposes. The sight of the Virgin and the Holy Child in a tavern window surrounded by whisky bottles is not uncommon at the Christmas season in the large cities.

The sum of all this is that religion today is not transforming the people; rather it is being transformed by the people. It is not raising the moral level of society; it is descending to society's own level and congratulating itself that it has scored a victory because society is smilingly accepting its surrender.

What too many religious leaders are overlooking is that the faith of Christ makes no concessions, accepts no compromises, allows no terms and makes no deals. Christ offers Himself to men as Lord and Savior and receives returning sinners only when they turn against themselves and come fully over on God's side. Fallen men escape the judgment of the world as Lot escaped the destruction of Sodom, by forsaking it altogether, not by getting adjusted to it.

The current vogue religion never says, "Thou shalt not;" that would be negative thinking and contrary to the best psychology. It does not command men; it smiles and cajoles and suggests and ends by letting the man have his own way. Anything goes as long as a sop is tossed to God in the form of "devotions" after the unreconstructed rebel has had his fun. God thus becomes a servant who stands ready to help in a pinch but who will not make any embarrassing demands or expect anyone to live a life much different from the customary easy life made familiar by the radio and the public press.

Undoubtedly here and there a happy exception may be found. The Holy Spirit has His few, as indeed He has always had, and their holy walk and tear-drenched prayers may yet save the day.

Are We Having a Revival of True Religion? Part VI

In the darkest days of Israel's history God never left Himself without a witness. Even when the worship of Baal was supreme in the land there were "seven thousand" who remained true to Jehovah (1 Kings 19:18).

It is a matter of deep personal gratification to me that I can and do believe that there is even in these degenerate times an elect remnant which seeks to know and do the will of God at any cost. And there is a slight possibility that that remnant may be larger today than it was a few years ago. I pray that I may have underestimated the number of the truly saved and that things may be brighter than I think. But making all allowance for what may be a too low view of the matter and drawing upon all Christian hopefulness and charity, I still cannot accept the idea that we in the United States are enjoying today a revival of the true Christian faith. A widely quoted British magazine about a year ago informed the world that we in America were indeed experiencing a "religious revival amounting to a social revolution." It is hard to imagine a more erroneous report, though undoubtedly it was published in good faith. The editors made the mistake of printing encouraging rumors without checking on the truth of them.

A genuine revival would raise the moral standards of society; instead, those standards are at a dismally low level everywhere. A genuine revival would check the divorce rate and bring back the sanctity of the home; instead, the divorce rate is higher than ever and the home is becoming little more than a place to sleep and watch television. A revival of true religion would discourage crime and juvenile delinquency; instead, the crime rate is higher than at any time in our history and youthful gang wars have become major police problems in our large cities.

Were the faith of our fathers exercising a major influence in society there would be a revolution in moral values among all Christians and a change in the outlook of multitudes who, while not themselves Christians, would nevertheless feel the strong pressure of Christian ethics and ideals around them. So it was in Italy under Savonarola, in Geneva under Calvin, in Germany in the time of Luther, in the England of the Wesleys and on a smaller scale in many places where revivals have broken out in cities and communities over the past centuries.

But in America no such change is found. The present flair for religion has not made people heavenly minded; rather it has secularized religion and put its approval upon the carnal values of fallen men. It glorifies success and eagerly prints religious testimonials from big corporation tycoons, actors, athletes, politicians and very important persons of every kind regardless of their reputation or lack of one. Religion is promoted by the identical techniques used to sell cigarettes. You pray to soothe your nerves just as you smoke to regain your composure after a sharp business transaction or a tight athletic contest. Books are written by the scores to show that Jesus is a Regular Fellow and Christianity a wise use of the highest psychological laws. All the holy principles of the Sermon on the Mount are present in reverse. Not the meek are blessed, but the self-important; not they that mourn but they that smile and smile and smile. Not the poor in spirit are dear to God, but they who are accounted somebody by the secular press. Not they that hunger and thirst after righteousness are filled, but they that hunger for publicity.

If I were describing only the nonevangelical religions the whole thing would not be so shocking. The fact is that the most popular gospel groups are deeply affected with this antigospel decay. To a tragic degree evangelical Christianity is now scriptural only in name. It has a name to live but is dead.

This has been an honest effort to understand the religious situation in the present critical hour. It is not meant as a denunciation, but as an appraisal. Surely there are a few names even today who have not defiled their garments and they shall walk with God in white, for they are worthy. Possibly we are coming near to a time when those who are on the Lord's side may be forced to withdraw from the religious hodgepodge and form a company of believers that will insist upon New Testament doctrine and New Testament practice. The temple waits to be cleansed. We should pray day and night till that happy event takes place.

No Competition

It is inherent in the nature of the religion of Christ that it cannot be promoted by competitive acts.

The essence of Christianity is selfless love. This was expressed first by our Lord in His redemptive suffering and has been expressed again and again since in every artless deed of kindness done by His followers for each other and for a suffering world. The essence of competition is self-love. Men compete to gain something for themselves, and in doing so they must of necessity cause someone else to lose what they gain. From this we gather that the two spirits are opposed to each other. We cannot be selfish and selfless at the same time.

Nothing spiritual can be gained in competition. The very idea of struggling with another for some eternal treasure of the soul is unthinkable. John

D. Rockefeller used to enjoy throwing a handful of shiny new dimes to a crowd of children and watching them scramble after them, each one struggling to grab as many as possible. The gifts and graces of God are not thus obtained. Each one of God's children can have all of Him and no one need receive less because another receives an abundance.

When two men step into a prize ring they know that only one can win, and whoever wins can do so only by forcing the other to lose. When five men line up on the track for a race they know that only one can come in first. Four men must lose that one may win. It is not so in the kingdom of God. Christians do not run against each other. All can win the race. Paul likens a Christian to a fighter, but the Christian's fight is not with other Christians. Each one can win and no one need lose. The man of faith fights against the devil, the flesh and the world. He wins as they lose; but he never wins anything truly spiritual in competition with a fellow believer. In the nature of things he cannot. To think so is to entertain an absurdity.

Whatever religious activity is, or even can be, promoted in a spirit of competition is of the flesh and must perish with the flesh; in the day of Christ nothing will remain but self-reproach and disappointment. Yet there are forms of religious promotion that lend themselves to selfish uses. The earthly scaffoldings of the Christian faith are often constructed from motives no higher than jealousy and personal ambition. The eternal part is above the reach of carnal men; the temporal elements are subject to the manipulations of ambitious leaders who seek glory for themselves. And verily they have their reward.

Circumstances being what they are the Christian minister is the one most tempted to carry on competitive religious activity. Even where his self-respect and good taste will not allow him to engage in an obvious race for numbers or publicity or fame he may yet harbor the spirit of envy within his heart and so be as guilty as the coarser and less inhibited bellwether who openly seeks to excel. He can get deliverance from the spirit of religious rivalry by going straight to God and having an understanding about the whole thing. Let him humble himself in the presence of God and in all earnestness pray somewhat like this:

Dear Lord, I refuse henceforth to compete with any of Thy servants. They have congregations larger than mine. So be it. I rejoice in their success. They have greater gifts. Very well. That is not in their power nor in mine. I am humbly grateful for their greater gifts and my smaller ones. I only pray that I may use to Thy glory such modest gifts as I possess. I will not compare myself with any, nor try to build up my self-esteem by noting where I may excel one or another in Thy holy work. I herewith make a blanket disavowal of all intrinsic worth. I am but an unprofitable servant. I gladly go to the foot of the class and own myself the least of Thy people. If I err in my self-judgment and actually underestimate myself I do not want to know it. I purpose to pray for others and to rejoice in their prosperity as if it were my own. And indeed it is my own if it is Thine own, for what is Thine is mine, and while one plants and another waters it is Thou alone that giveth the increase.

The man who walks according to the spirit of this prayer will find himself free from all envy and all rivalry and will be at liberty to serve God in the simplicity and power of the Holy Ghost. Such a man will build with gold and silver and precious stones and will escape the tragedy of discovering too late that he has built of wood, hay and stubble.

CHAPTER

30

We Must Think Right If We Would Be Right

What we think about when we are free to think about what we will—that is what we are or will soon become.

The Bible has a great deal to say about our thoughts; current evangelicalism has practically nothing to say about them. The reason the Bible says so much is that our thoughts are so vitally important to us; the reason evangelicalism says so little is that we are overreacting from the "thought" cults, such as New Thought, Unity, Christian Science and their like. These cults make our thoughts to be very nearly everything and we counter by making them very nearly nothing. Both positions are wrong.

Our voluntary thoughts not only reveal what we are, they predict what we will become. Except for that conduct which springs from our basic nat- *all conscious behavior...* ural instincts, all conscious behavior is preceded by and arises out of our thoughts. The will can be- come a servant of the thoughts, and to a large de- gree even our emotions follow our thinking. "The more I think about it the madder I get" is the way the average man states it, and in so doing not only reports accurately on his own mental processes but pays as well an unconscious tribute to the power of thought. Thinking stirs feeling and feel- — *note* ing triggers action. That is the way we are made and we may as well accept it.

The psalms and prophets contain numerous ref- erences to the power of right thinking to raise reli- gious feeling and incite to right conduct. "I thought on my ways, and turned my feet unto thy testimo- nies" (Psalm 119:59). "While I was musing the fire burned: then spake I with my tongue" (39:3). Over and over the Old Testament writers exhort us to get quiet and think about high and holy things as a pre- liminary to amendment of life or a good deed or a courageous act.

The Old Testament is not alone in its respect for the God-given power of human thought. Christ taught that men defile themselves by evil thinking and even went so far as to equate a thought with an act: "That whosoever looketh on a woman to lust af- ter her hath committed adultery with her already in his heart" (Matthew 5:28). Paul recited a list of shin- ing virtues and commanded, "Think on these things" (Philippians 4:8).

These quotations are but four out of hundreds that could be cited from the Scriptures. Thinking about God and holy things creates a moral climate favorable to the growth of faith and love and humility and reverence. We cannot by thinking regenerate our hearts, nor take our sins away nor change the leopard's spots. Neither can we by thinking add one cubit to our stature or make evil good or darkness light. So to teach is to misrepresent a scriptural truth and to use it to our own undoing. But we can by Spirit-inspired thinking help to make our minds pure sanctuaries in which God will be pleased to dwell.

I referred in a previous paragraph to "our voluntary thoughts" and I used the words advisedly. In our journey through this evil and hostile world many thoughts will be forced upon us which we do not like and for which we have no moral sympathy. The necessity to make a living may compel us for days on end to entertain thoughts in no sense elevating. Ordinary awareness of the doings of our fellow men will bring thoughts repugnant to our Christian souls. These need affect us but little. For them we are not responsible and they may pass through our minds like a bird through the air, without leaving a trace. They have no lasting effect upon us because they are not our own. They are unwelcome intruders for which we have no love and which we get rid of as quickly as possible.

Anyone who wishes to check on his true spiritual condition may do so by noting what his voluntary thoughts have been over the last hours or days.

What has he thought about when free to think of what he pleased? Toward what has his inner heart turned when it was free to turn where it would? When the bird of thought was let go did it fly out like the raven to settle upon floating carcasses or did it like the dove circle and return again to the ark of God? Such a test is easy to run, and if we are honest with ourselves we can discover not only what we are but what we are going to become. We'll soon be the sum of our voluntary thoughts.

While our thoughts stir our feelings, and thus strongly influence our wills, it is yet true that the will can be and should be master of our thoughts. Every normal person can determine what he will think about. Of course the troubled or tempted man may find his thoughts somewhat difficult to control and even while he is concentrating upon a worthy object, wild and fugitive thoughts may play over his mind like heat lightning on a summer evening. These are likely to be more bothersome than harmful and in the long run do not make much difference one way or another.

The best way to control our thoughts is to offer the mind to God in complete surrender. The Holy Spirit will accept it and take control of it immediately. Then it will be relatively easy to think on spiritual things, especially if we train our thoughts by long periods of daily prayer. Long practice in the art of mental prayer (that is, talking to God inwardly as we work or travel) will help to form the habit of holy thought.

The best way of all is to "let this mind be in you, which was also in Christ Jesus" (Philippians 2:5). For to have the mind of Christ is to have good and pure thoughts always.

Not Moses, But Abraham

The Christian's spiritual progenitor is not Moses but Abraham.

The great doctrine of faith takes us back to Abraham and thus antedates the Law of Moses by 430 years. This is the argument of Paul in Galatians 3:15-18 and Romans 4:9-16.

There is a mistaken notion abroad that in the Old Testament salvation came by obedience to the Law, while in the New Testament it comes by faith. The truth is that since the beginning of the world no one was ever saved in any way other than by grace through faith.

"The law was given by Moses, but grace and truth came by Jesus Christ" (John 1:17). But grace and truth came by Jesus Christ long before the incarnation. When God slew those beasts (presumably lambs) and gave the skins to Adam and Eve for clothing He was telling them in symbolic language that the redemption of the race would be by the merit of innocent life laid down. Not by law but by atonement would they and their descendants be ransomed from the Fall.

This idea was never wholly lost to mankind. When the Law was given it was accompanied by a system of sin offerings and atoning sacrifices leading straight to the Savior who was to come. When John pointed to Jesus and exclaimed, "Behold the Lamb of God, which taketh away the sin of the world" (John 1:29), he was identifying Christ with all the sacrificial lambs that had been offered for sin from the time of Abel to the appearance of Emmanuel.

The idea creeps into much evangelical teaching that the Old Testament is a book of justice and judgment without a ray of mercy or grace or love to lighten the darkness, whereas the New Testament is filled with mercy and forgiveness. The truth is that mercy and justice, love and judgment are found in both the Old and the New Testament in about equal proportion. Not two Gods but one wrote the Bible and the unity of His perfect character reveals itself in all parts of the Scriptures.

It may come as a surprise to some to learn that there is as much about mercy in the Old Testament as in the New, but such is actually the case. Grace is found throughout the Old Testament, and love also is found there in abundance. Justification by faith is an Old Testament doctrine. It was first associated with Abraham, appeared later in the writings of David and Habakkuk and was shown by Paul to be one of the most vital doctrines of the New Testament. Thus the organic unity of the Bible is confirmed.

It is a heartening thought that no one ever had or can have any advantage over another in his search for God. No matter what the dispensation or the circumstances, everyone who came to God came by faith. Those of ancient times looked forward to the cross and those of later times looked and must look back to it. Everyone and anyone may find forgiveness and cleansing through the grace of our Lord Jesus Christ, and any progress in the knowledge of God, any growth in spiritual stature must come the same way. Our spiritual ancestor is Abraham whose faith pleased God, brought an imputation of righteousness and made him the father of the faithful.

We Christians are the sons of faith and the heirs of liberty. Let us stand fast therefore in the liberty wherewith Christ has made us free.

The Value of a Good Home

The oldest institution in the world is the home. It had its beginning in the garden which the Lord God planted eastward in Eden, where also He placed the man and the woman whom He created.

Under such ideal conditions began the home, that sacred unit of human society which through the long centuries has gathered round its head like a coronet such riches of beautiful associations and undying memories.

Consider the home. From time immemorial it has been the focal point around which our kindest thoughts gather, a refuge for the troubled, a harbor for the storm-tossed, a resting place to which we may return when weary and oppressed by a world that has been too much for us. However humble its furnishings, however modest its size, there is always room there for the heart, its richest and its most beautiful appointment.

So perverse is human nature, so wayward the soul, that we may come to accept our childhood home as a matter of course and forget for a time what a treasure it was. But though we have strayed far from its hallowed precincts the time is sure to come when we remember it again with tender yearnings and regrets.

Let illness visit us or some heavy blow fall upon us to shake our confidence and stagger our minds: then in a flash we will remember. The heart will return home again like a dove to her window. Then will the loved faces smile once more and the voices that have been so long silent will be heard as plain as in the days of yore. In a moment the years roll back and the members of the little family group from which we have been separated so long by the miles and the years laugh together again. We recognize each friendly face, to us still young and still beautiful; we hear our nickname that we had all but forgotten and it is sweet and strange to hear it in our inner ear after the passing of the years. We know then, and confess in a rush of feeling, how precious was the time spent at home with our own people in peace before the grown-up lust for treasure or fame had lured us out into the wide world.

Impressions gained in childhood have greater power to shape our lives than anything we may learn in later years. Sometimes we are permitted to see how deeply men are affected by that first pre-school education gained as it were by accident in their childhood home. That elderly man who came to our shores while still a child and who has spoken the English language for the better part of his life-time lies down for his last sleep. Before his voice is lost in death he whispers a final prayer to his God and Father—not in the language of his adult years but in that of his motherland, first heard in the old home across the sea in the country of his birth. Life's beginnings return at its ending.

It is vitally important that our homes be pre-served. A nation is only as strong as its homes. No government can substitute for the ministrations of the family. Federal agencies cannot love and cuddle the baby, not kiss his bruised knee or hear his prayer at the close of the day. Fathers and mothers make homes; nothing else can. And whether our American homes produce delinquents or upright citizens will depend altogether upon what kind of fathers and mothers preside in those homes.

If the home is the oldest institution on earth the Church is the loftiest, and historically there has al-ways been a close relationship between the two. The family that stays close to the church is the one most likely to hold together. Churchgoing par-ents make churchgoing children, and while there may be an occasional exception, boys and girls brought up in Christian homes tend strongly to be good and law-abiding adults. The armies of crime do not draw their recruits from the church or Sunday school.

Police and juvenile authorities agree that the best guarantee against moral delinquency among young people is a good religious training. The example of serious-minded God-fearing persons is a tremendous power for good. Young people who have the blessing of association with earnest Christians in church and in the home have a powerful advantage over those who are reared away from the church.

The church cannot save the soul; but it can and does serve as an effective school of good living. In addition to the saving gospel which sounds forth from the pulpits of our true Christian churches, there is heard also instruction in righteousness, the value of honesty, purity and truthfulness and the superiority of the homely virtues. These things are treasures above rubies. No child should be deprived of the advantage they bring.

Parents who desire the best for their children should not overlook their spiritual nurture. To such parents we offer the following suggestions: Start taking your children to a good church regularly. Help them to get acquainted with others of their own ages within the fellowship of the church. Get them into the Sunday school, and then back up these efforts with family Bible reading. Above all, put your trust in Jesus Christ and set a good example in the home. You'll never regret that you did.

CHAPTER

33

Why We Are Lukewarm
about Christ's Return

Shortly after the close of the First World War, I heard a great Southern preacher say that he feared the intense interest in prophecy current at that time would result in a dying out of the blessed hope when events had proved the excited interpreters wrong.

The man was a prophet, or at least a remarkably shrewd student of human nature, for exactly what he predicted has come to pass. The hope of Christ's coming is today all but dead among evangelicals.

I do not mean that Bible Christians have given up the doctrine of the second advent. By no means. There has been, as every informed person knows, an adjustment among some of the lesser tenets of our prophetic credo, but the vast majority of evangelicals continue to hold to the belief that Jesus Christ will sometime actually come back to the earth in person. The ultimate triumph of Christ is accepted as one of the unshakable doctrines of Holy Scripture.

It is true that in some quarters the prophecies of the Bible are occasionally expounded. This is especially so among Hebrew Christians who, for reasons well understood, seem to feel closer to the prophets of the Old Testament than do Gentile believers. Their love for their own people naturally leads them to grasp at every hope of the conversion and ultimate restoration of Israel. To many of them the return of Christ represents a quick and happy solution of the "Jewish problem." The long centuries of wandering will end when He comes and God will at that time "restore again the kingdom to Israel" (Acts 1:6). We dare not allow our deep love for our Hebrew Christian brethren to blind us to the obvious political implications of this aspect of their Messianic hope. We do not blame them for this. We merely call attention to it.

Yet the return of Christ as a blessed hope is, as I said above, all but dead among us. The truth touching the second advent, where it is presented today, is for the most part either academic or political. The joyful personal element is altogether missing. Where are they who

> Yearn for the sign, O Christ, of Thy
>   fulfilling,
> Faint for the flaming of Thine advent feet?

The longing to see Christ that burned in the breasts of those first Christians seems to have burned itself out. All we have left are the ashes. It is precisely the "yearning" and the "fainting" for the return of Christ that has distinguished the personal hope from the theological one. Mere acquaintance with correct doctrine is a poor substitute for Christ and familiarity with New Testament eschatology will never take the place of a love-inflamed desire to look on His face.

If the tender yearning is gone from the advent hope today there must be a reason for it; and I think I know what it is, or what they are, for there are a number of them. One is simply that popular Fundamentalist theology has emphasized the utility of the cross rather than the beauty of the One who died on it. The saved man's relation to Christ has been made contractual instead of personal. The "work" of Christ has been stressed until it has eclipsed the person of Christ. Substitution has been allowed to supersede identification. What He *did for me* seems to be more important than what He *is to me*. Redemption is seen as an across-the-counter transaction which we "accept," and the whole thing lacks emotional content. We must love someone very much to stay awake and long for his coming, and that may explain the absence of power in the advent hope even among those who still believe in it.

Another reason for the absence of real yearning for Christ's return is that Christians are so comfortable in this world that they have little desire to leave it. For those leaders who set the pace of religion and determine its content and quality, Christianity has become of late remarkably lucrative. The streets of gold do not have too great an appeal for those who find it so easy to pile up gold and silver in the service of the Lord here on earth. We all want to reserve the hope of heaven as a kind of insurance against the day of death, but as long as we are healthy and comfortable, why change a familiar good for something about which we know very little actually? So reasons the carnal mind, and so subtly that we are scarcely aware of it.

Again, in these times religion has become jolly good fun right here in this present world, and what's the hurry about heaven anyway? Christianity, contrary to what some had thought, is another and higher form of entertainment. Christ has done all the suffering. He has shed all the tears and carried all the crosses; we have but to enjoy the benefits of His heartbreak in the form of religious pleasures modeled after the world but carried on in the name of Jesus. So say the same people who claim to believe in Christ's second coming.

History reveals that times of suffering for the Church have also been times of looking upward. Tribulation has always sobered God's people and encouraged them to look for and yearn after the return of their Lord. Our present preoccupation with this world may be a warning of bitter days to come. God will wean us from the earth some way—the easy way if possible, the hard way if necessary. It is up to us.

CHAPTER

34

On Omitting That
Third Stanza

One of the commonest expressions heard in the public worship service is the leader's directive, "Sing the first, second and last verses;" or, "Omit the third verse, please."

Now, we'll overlook the fact that the director obviously means *stanza* and not *verse*. We are all so prone to inaccuracies of speech that it does not become any of us to be too hard on the rest of us, though it would seem that any man who accepts a position that places him before the public should inform himself on matters with which that position requires that he be familiar.

I suppose it is not of vast importance that the third stanza is so often omitted in the singing of a hymn, but just for the record let it be said that the worshipers are deprived of the blessing of the hymn by that omission if, as is often true, the hymn develops a great Christian truth in sermonic outline. To omit a stanza is to lose one link in a golden chain and greatly to reduce the value of the whole hymn.

The significant thing, however, is not what the omission actually does, but what it suggests, viz., a nervous impatience and a desire to get the service over with. We are, for instance, singing "When I Survey the Wondrous Cross." We long to forget the big noisy world and let our hearts go out in reverent worship of that Prince of Glory who died for us, but our sad sweet longing is killed in the bud by the brisk, unemotional voice of the director ordering us to "omit the third verse." We wonder vaguely whether the brother is hungry or has to catch an early train or just why he is so anxious to get through with the hymn. Since all standard hymns have been edited to delete inferior stanzas and since any stanza of the average hymn can be sung in less than one minute ("When I Survey the Wondrous Cross" clocks at thirty seconds to the stanza, normal tempo!) and since many of our best hymns have already been shortened as much as good taste will allow, we are forced to conclude that the habit of omitting the third stanza reveals religious boredom, pure and simple, and it would do our souls good if we would admit it.

If it were only in our hymn singing that this spirit were found I would probably not have brought the matter up at all, but I find it in pretty near every department of the religious life. Not the doing of evil deeds only but the omission of good deeds weakens the soul and invites the judgments of God. The same worldly, impatient spirit that shortens a hymn also shortens our prayer time and reduces the amount we give to the Lord's work, as well as the number of services we attend each week.

There is always danger that God may intend to speak to us at a gathering of the saints, and we thwart the loving purposes of God for us by not being present at the time of visitation. A wise old deacon said to the young Evan Roberts, "Now, lad, be sure to attend every prayer meeting. God may want to bless you sometime and you will miss it because you are not present. Remember Thomas and what he missed because he wasn't there." Evan never forgot that exhortation. He never missed a prayer meeting from that day on. And it is significant that it was in a prayer meeting that God touched Evan Roberts and the great Welsh revival began.

There have been devotional writers (for example, some of the so-called "mystic" theologians) who held that sin is at bottom a negation, an absence of something, a no-thing, and that its destructive power lies right there. God, they said, is the Something, the positive Entity, and evil is the repudiation of God, the denial in thought and deed of the Eternal Something that we know to be the Lord God Almighty, Maker of heaven and earth. This would appear to be too rarefied, too one-sided a concept to account for sin as the Bible and the world know it. Yet there is more than a modicum of truth in it. How much of evil is omission! "Therefore to him that knoweth to do good, and doeth it not, to him it is sin" (James 4:17).

It may be that sins of omission are the worst sins of all. Dr. R.A. Torrey said that if the first and greatest commandment is to love God with all our hearts, the greatest sin is to fail to love Him. If Torrey was correct, then the darkest sin in the world is a negation, a no-thing, something men do not do. Finney preached great sermons on the sins of omission. Every Christian has felt the sharp sting of conscience over deeds not done, and sometimes the sense of guilt is greater than for wrongs committed.

The moral man who boasts that he has never lied or cheated or harmed his fellow man may be in for a shock in the day of judgment. Not to have done a positive good is to have done evil. Not to be where we should have been is as bad as to be where we should not be. To be absent when the Lord distributes His blessings may easily prove to be a real tragedy. Not to pray when we should pray is like failing to open a letter full of good news. The loss is too great to estimate.

Let's sing the third stanza.

Let's Face the Facts

A few days ago I heard a man speak on First Corinthians 13, the familiar love chapter of the New Testament. His message pointed up a modern heresy against which I have often warned and about which I now consider it my duty to write a few words.

The preacher was not a cultist, but an evangelical and a Fundamentalist. Undoubtedly, he would have given his right eye rather than teach false doctrine or otherwise injure the souls of his hearers. Nevertheless, I believe he was injuring them and teaching false doctrine into the bargain.

The heart of his message appeared to be that the description of love in that Corinthian chapter applies to our Lord Jesus Christ. And of course it was easy to prove that it does. "Christ suffereth long, and is kind; Christ envieth not; Christ vaunteth not Himself, is not puffed up, Doth not behave Himself unseemly, seeketh not His own, is not easily provoked, thinketh no evil . . ." and so to the end of the chapter.

Now, no Christian would deny that Jesus Christ, being very God of very God, has in Himself all moral virtues in full perfection. God is love and Christ is God, so it follows that anything that can be said of love can be said also of Christ. But to make Paul's words describe Christ is to read into them a meaning Paul never intended, which of course is to introduce error into the interpretation of Scripture. And the error is not one of interpretation merely; it has practical and serious consequences in that it ignores the solemn warning of the chapter and relieves us of all obligation to seek and obtain the love of God in our own hearts.

Just what is Paul telling us in this 13th chapter of his first Corinthian epistle? That love is absolutely indispensable to the Christian life. The gift of tongues without love is so much noise. The gift of prophecy without love is of no benefit. Without love, knowledge and faith are useless. And though a man bestow all his goods to feed the poor and die at last a martyr's death, if he have not love it profits him nothing. So Paul states in the first three verses, after which he describes love and identifies it so the reader will know what kind of person he must be to escape an unprofitable, empty and deceived existence.

Paul's analysis of love is not intended to tell us what kind of being Christ is, but *what kind of person a real Christian must be*. That these virtues are all in

Christ, I repeat, is the common belief of all Christians, but they were not listed in the inspired Word to teach us that. So to hold and teach is to play a shoddy trick on our own souls and on the souls of our hearers.

Perhaps a homemade illustration may help. What does "health" mean for a man? Well, it means a pulse rate of 72, a body temperature of 98.6 degrees, a blood count of 5,000 white cells and 5,000,000 red cells per cubic millimeter, a respiration rate of 20 at rest, 30 percent solids to 70 percent water body composition, and so on. Any doctor could carry this on until he had described the man of ideal health.

The 13th chapter of First Corinthians may tell us what Christ is like, but let us not forget that it also tells us what we must be like to avoid spiritual tragedy. Let us not turn our back on this critically important teaching. Without love, the kind described by Paul, my whole Christian life is a barren fig tree. It's a neat trick to apply Paul's words to Christ only; but it isn't honest and it is dangerous.

It is the Holy Spirit who sheds abroad the love of God in our hearts (Romans 5:5) and love is declared to be a fruit of the Spirit (Galatians 5:22). But if our daily lives reveal that the fruit is not there we dare not assume that it is— "because the Bible says so." The absence of love as described in First Corinthians 13 is proof of the absence of the Spirit, or at least that He is inoperative within us. That's the only honest conclusion. We can't afford to be less than candid about the whole thing.

"What Does It Take to Thrill a Man?"

A great city newspaper came up lately with an idea that might have meaning to a lot of us Christians any time and seems to be especially appropriate around the Thanksgiving season.

Asking the question, "What does it take to thrill a man?" the editorial writer said that a man whose name is known throughout the whole world, who has received from the nations of the earth just about every honor that can be accorded to men and whose own country had elected him to the highest position it could give any of its citizens, had recently expressed himself as being "thrilled" at being permitted to sit up a few minutes in a wheel chair. That man, of course, was Dwight D. Eisenhower, and the occasion was his first time out of bed after his heart attack.

This touching incident in the life of a great man should teach us that we are likely to overlook our real blessings and fail to be thankful for them because they are small or because they appear to be trifling and ordinary. We may be grateful for life's rare mountain peaks and fail completely to see the dozens or scores of little hills that make the landscape beautiful.

Biography may be either a help or a hindrance, depending upon how we interpret and apply it. The biographer usually accents the high, stirring moments in the life of his subject and of necessity passes over the days and years when nothing out of the ordinary happened. Yet without the thousands of common days there could have been no continuity between the uncommon ones to bind the life together. In reading the lives of great men we must beware that we do not become dissatisfied with our tame existence and hold lightly the countless treasures which through the mercy of God we all possess. A life that lasted fifty or seventy or ninety years must be condensed into a few pages with the result that the terrain is shoved together and the view distorted. From this out-of-focus picture we are likely to draw three erroneous conclusions: one, that the subject was greater than he actually was; two, that by contrast we are smaller than we really are, and three, that God respects persons and distributes His favors unevenly among His children.

Everything in life is relative, including our blessings. A man who has had the world at his feet may be reduced to a state where he will be grateful for the privilege of sitting fifteen minutes in a wheel chair. And the man thus placed who can be as grateful for one gift as for the other has learned the true meaning of Thanksgiving. A man who has been for years totally blind may laugh and weep with thankfulness if at last he recovers but partial sight in one eye. The little polio victim will scream with delight when he discovers that he can run a little bit, even if in doing so he must push an awkward brace along with him. And so with all our lives and all our days. We are always richer than we think.

The conclusion of the matter is simply that we should cultivate the habit of being thankful for small things. Not that we should be less grateful for the great epochal blessings, such as our first radiant sight of the shining kingdom of God in conversion, or deliverance from some physical disease in answer to prayer. These great mountain peaks will always command our attention and stir our hearts to praise. But we must see to it that we do not ignore the humbler blessings.

Personally I am not as strong as Samson, but I'll never cease to thank God I am able to get about over the surface of the earth and attend to the work God has given me to do. I am not a Plato mentally, but I thank God I am sane. I am not rich, but neither am I reduced to beggary. And so with every other blessing the Lord has given me. I hope always to be thankful for the little things; then I'll know what to do with the big ones when God sees fit to send them my way.

God's Blessings Are
Found in "The Way"

"I being in the way" [explained
Eliezer], "the LORD led me."
(Genesis 24:27)

more than one
meaning:
① being a hindrance
② living in obedience to the Lord — "the Way"
it's the second that is meant here.

The circumstances were these: When Abraham was old and well stricken in age he called to him his faithful servant Eliezer and commissioned him to go on a long journey into Mesopotamia to procure a wife for Isaac, Abraham's well-beloved son. This was in the far-seeing plan of God and required a man of real faith and consecration to carry it out. The man must have unusual wisdom that he might be led to the right place and fix on the right girl. It looked like a difficult and complicated task, too much indeed for any man to accomplish, but Eliezer came through victoriously. He simply obeyed and God did the rest. He took the appointed way and the Lord led him. It was as simple as that.

Three hundred years later God said to Israel, "Behold, I send an Angel before thee, to keep thee in the way, and to bring thee into the place which I have prepared" (Exodus 23:20). Throughout the Old Testament and on into the New a way is set before men, and over that way the angel of the Lord hovers day and night, guarding and blessing all who faithfully walk in it. They have only to stay in the ordained path to assure the continued fellowship of God.

God's blessing follows the "way" as green vegetation the river. God never varies from the way; He never compromises nor approves a detour. There is just one way, no more, and our present success and future happiness depend upon our finding and following that way.

In the Scriptures the Lord is pictured as a Shepherd walking before His sheep, leading them through the dangerous wilderness of this world. Yet in Isaiah 30:21 it is written, "And thine ears shall hear a word behind thee, saying, This is the way, walk ye in it." Why does the voice of the Lord sound from *behind* us instead of coming as usual from before? The rest of the verse makes it clear, "*when ye turn to the right hand, and when ye turn to the left.*" Whenever we turn our backs on the way, the voice comes from behind us. The Lord never leaves the way. Always His voice sounds in the way and if we wander from it we can only hear a voice behind us, never in front.

The story of the rich young ruler illustrates this further. As Christ watched the young ruler walk away from Him He could speak only from behind him. And as the distance between the two increased, so much more faintly sounded the voice of Jesus in the young man's ears. That was and could be only tragedy for the erring man. Christ calls men to Him. He never leaves the true way to go to them.

Most of the troubles of Christians result from their leaving the way of the Lord to walk in paths of their own choosing. This is justified on the grounds that it is merely an adaptation to the times, a wise adjustment to the changing tastes of modern men. Paul's words, "I am made all things to all men, that I might by all means save some" (1 Corinthians 9:22), are lifted out of context and used to give apostolic authority to a bewildering variety of religious frivolities of which prophet or apostle never dreamed. Christians find themselves on unscriptural bypaths far from the plain way of the cross and, assuming they are on the right way, they pray day and night for God to lead them and bless their journey. But their prayers are worse than wasted. By leaving the way of the Lord they cut themselves off from divine assistance. No amount of frantic pleading can save them from disaster.

We can save ourselves a lot of desperate praying for help that never comes if we will but obey the plain teachings of the Scriptures and walk in the way they point out for us. We congratulate ourselves these days that we are more "enlightened" than were those rugged old men of Bible times, but I think we can learn a lot from the man who, more than 3,500 years ago, testified, "I being in the way, . . . the Lord led me."

The Last Sin to Go

The desire for social approbation is one of the less odious self-sins. It has about it nothing of the offensive quality of, say, self-love or self-righteousness. Under certain circumstances it might even be a virtue, for if the world were populated with men and women of pure hearts and holy lives it would be right and natural to want to live in such a manner as to earn their approval.

Undoubtedly those holy beings that inhabit the world above take pleasure in the love and respect of their fellow creatures, but there is and can be no moral parallel between heaven and earth. We dwell in a world halfway between heaven and hell. In hell there is only evil; in heaven there is only good; on earth the tares and wheat grow together, with the tares vastly outnumbering the wheat. There was at least one period in the history of the world when the righteous could be numbered on the fingers of both hands, not counting the thumbs, and the language of Christ gives strong reason to believe that the proportion of good and evil will not be much different at the end of the age (Matthew 24:37–39; Luke 17:26–30).

So corrupt is human nature, so ungodly and rebellious the race of mankind, that the true friend of God is not likely to be accepted by the world, though it sometimes happens that he will be praised for doing something of benefit to society, such, for instance, as the opening up of the interior of Africa by David Livingstone. But the more Christlike men become the surer they are to feel the force of our Lord's words: "If ye were of the world, the world would love his own: but because ye are not of the world, but I have chosen you out of the world, therefore the world hateth you" (John 15:19); and the words of Paul: "Yea, and all that will live godly in Christ Jesus shall suffer persecution" (2 Timothy 3:12).

To be a true Christian requires that we agree to forfeit the approval of the world. Yet so human are we that this desire to please our fellow men remains with us long after other sins have departed. Mostly we compromise the matter by narrowing the circle of persons whose approval we seek. We write off the sinful worldling as impossible to please and give ourselves no concern about whether or not he approves us. Along with him go the liberal, the modernist, the cultist and a host of others like him. Then we begin to congratulate ourselves that we "fear the face of no man," that we are fearless cross-carrying saints who care nothing for the blame or the praise of men.

Maybe so, but where is the Christian who is actually dead to public opinion? For the most part we are merely dead to the opinion of certain sections of the public, and have preserved to ourselves other smaller groups whose opinion we value very much indeed. I have noticed how this tendency runs throughout all human society. The "highbrow" scorns the favor of the vast majority of mankind, but eagerly courts the favor of his little circle of fellow highbrows and is broken-hearted if they frown upon him. The "society" woman appears to care nothing for the opinion of the millions who read about her shady escapades, but would be driven to suicide if she were excluded from the narrow but select group whose esteem she has come to depend upon as her very life and breath.

Among Christians things are not much different. A preacher earns the reputation of being "fearless" by attacking liberals, Catholics, liquor and immorality, but fawns at the feet of his own little group. He may boldly insult the Pope, but would never dare to cross the monied deacon in his congregation nor express a theological opinion which he knew to be contrary to the mass opinion of the religious group with whom he associates. He is perfectly willing to make enemies of everyone who does not share the opinions of his denomination, but he is careful not to offend anyone in the denomination who is in a position to make him suffer for it.

I cannot believe in the spirituality of any Christian man who keeps an eye open for the approval of others, whoever they may be. The man after God's own heart must be dead to the opinion of his friends as well as his enemies. He must be as willing to cross important persons as obscure ones. He must be ready to rebuke his superior as quickly as those who may be beneath him on the ecclesiastical ladder. To reprove one man in order to gain the favor of another is no evidence of moral courage. It is done in the world all the time.

We'll never be where we should be in our spiritual lives until we are so devoted to Christ that we ask no other approbation than His smile. When we are wholly lost in Him the frantic effort to please men will come to an end. The circle of persons we struggle to please will be narrowed to One. Then we will know true freedom, but not a moment before.

CHAPTER

39

Such Wise Men Are Too Rare

Not much is known about the wise men who came out of the East in search of the newborn King of the Jews, but everything that is known is good. They were "wise men" indeed and checked well on every count.

As far as we know, these men did not have the advantage of a written revelation as did the Jews. They only felt after God in hope that they might find Him, and by His infinite goodness they did find Him. By the dim light of nature, aided perhaps by a tradition borrowed from the Jews, they learned that a Redeemer-King was to come out of Israel and their hearts conceived a great longing to worship Him and to lay some gift at His feet.

Imperfect and sketchy as their faith must have been, God honored it and whispered to them the wondrous news of the approaching Advent. That they were not mere ivory-tower religious dreamers is proved by the fact that they immediately set out to make the long journey, determined to follow the star till it led them to the Savior. Theirs is a good example, and their story a noble and heartening one to meditate upon in this day of universal religious lethargy.

So rich is this story, so replete with lofty and elevating details, that it has been read and told for 20 centuries without exhausting its treasures or dulling the shining luster that surrounds it. Each hearer finds in it something new and fresh each time it is told. But to me at this approaching Christmas season the story of the wise men says two things and says them loudly.

One is that *a longing soul with scanty theological knowledge is in a better position to meet God than a self-satisfied soul, however deeply instructed in the Scriptures.*

The wise men were Gentiles, "being aliens from the commonwealth of Israel, and strangers from the covenants of promise, having no hope, and without God in the world." Yet they saw the star and left all to make the long, dangerous journey to lay worthy gifts at the feet of Jesus. They acted on small knowledge and found the Messiah. That is to their everlasting credit.

On the other hand there were in those days chief priests, high priests, scribes, lawyers, rulers of the synagogues—all keen-eyed students of the Scriptures and experts in the Law and the Prophets; yet as far as we know not one of them had any spiritual awareness that the great day of Israel's visitation had come. They could tell the wise men instantly what the prophets had written about the birthplace of the King, but their knowledge was formal merely. They themselves were blind to its real meaning. Gentiles had to come and rouse them from their strange stupor, if indeed they were ever aroused, for there is little evidence to show that they understood the wise men or knew what all the excitement was about.

The second message the story brings is that *the wise men came to Jesus not to gain something from Him but to give something to Him.*

This circumstance is so unusual as to be almost incredible. We must shake our heads to dispel the clouds from our minds and wait a moment to let our thoughts clear before we can grasp such an idea. It is all so contrary to everything we have been hearing all our lives. Imagine coming to Christ with any other motive than to gain something from Him!

This one act stands almost alone in the life of our Lord. Almost, I say, but not quite, for Mary later broke the alabaster box and poured the precious ointment on His head, and after His crucifixion the two Marys came to look for Him; asking nothing, expecting nothing, but impelled by a selfless love they came to bear His body away. Beyond this there is little evidence of anything as pure and lofty as the worship offered by the wise men. Possibly there was more than we know, and charity would dictate that we at least hope that there was.

One thing that makes the act of unselfish worship appear so beautiful is that it is so rare. Apparently the people of Jesus' day thought of Him as a
source of help merely, and it is the "merely" that
makes the whole thing questionable. A source of
help He was indeed, a fountain in the desert, a star
to guide the mariner, bread for the hungry, health
for the afflicted and everything that fallen and sinful man can need. Yes, He is our helper, but not our
helper *merely*. He is our Lord and our God as well,
and infinitely worthy of our ardent, poured-out
love and devotion altogether apart from anything
He may do for us.

While Christ walked on earth many came to Him,
and the motives that brought them were almost as
many as they who came. They sought to make Him
a king for political gain; they sought preferment for
personal ends, as the brothers James and John.
They came for healing, for deliverance, for help for
themselves, their children and their friends. Among
these motives, if some were questionable, others
were good and legitimate, but none was wholly free
from selfishness of a sort.

Once a leper came to Jesus. In his great distress he
could think of only one thing—getting rid of his re-
pulsive sores and becoming a well man again. He
came because he wanted something, and the Lord
understood and gave it to him. His motive was not
the highest, but it was acceptable. Later he came
back with a heart full of gratitude and fell on his face
to worship Jesus. The first pleased the Lord, no
doubt, but the second pleased Him more.

CHAPTER

40

Sure! Pay That Income Tax

A reader of *The Alliance Weekly* (now *Alliance Life*) writes to inquire about the federal income tax. Her question is right to the point, "Should we pay it or not?"

It had never occurred to me that there could be any doubt in anyone's mind about the Christian's obligation toward the income tax, but if one person is troubled about it maybe there are others, so here are a few thoughts, as the political orators say, "along that line."

Spies, feigning themselves just men, once came to Jesus with the question, "Is it lawful to give tribute unto Caesar, or not?" (Matthew 22:17). These spies were obviously using an honest question to entrap our Lord. The problem they brought to the Savior was one that had been bothering a lot of good people and if it had been asked in sincerity would have been altogether right and proper. Our Lord with His amazing penetration answered the question for all men of good will—and did it without falling into the trap so carefully set for Him.

His answer has become celebrated. "Render therefore unto Caesar the things which are Caesar's; and unto God the things that are God's" (Matthew 22:21). Neither the Romans nor the Jewish authorities could object to this injunction, since no one would dare to admit he wanted anything that was not his.

Anyway the word stands, render to governmental authorities whatever by legal right belongs to them. And since they determine what is legally theirs, it is the duty of the Christian to pay—withholding only that over which earthly powers have no right, viz., worship, supreme love and the moral and spiritual claims of the Most High God. These are the things that belong to God alone; and where earthly governments infringe upon them it is and always will be the sacred obligation of every Christian to resist to the death.

Since it is usually not good practice to rest an entire case upon one passage of Scripture, look also at Paul's words to the Roman Christians:

> Let every soul be subject unto the higher powers. For there is no power but of God: the powers that be are ordained of God. Whosoever therefore resisteth the power, resisteth the ordinance of God: and they that resist shall receive to themselves dam-

nation . . . Wherefore ye must needs be subject, not only for wrath, but also for conscience sake. For for this cause pay ye tribute also: for they are God's ministers, attending continually upon this very thing. Render therefore to all their dues: tribute to whom tribute is due; custom to whom custom; fear to whom fear; honour to whom honour. (Romans 13:1-2, 5-7)

When we remember that "tribute" is *taxes* and is so rendered in many translations, the question of whether or not a Christian should pay his income tax seems no longer to be in doubt. The answer of Christ and Paul is, Yes.

While human governments ("the powers that be") are ordained of God, it does not follow that the rulers or officials of a given country are therefore always just and wise. They can and do err in their judgments and often impose ordinances that are anything but judicious and levy taxes unreasonably high.

It is my opinion that our present federal income tax will prove in the long run to work against the interests of the country. It is altogether possible for a nation to tax itself out of existence. Taxes are absolutely necessary as being the only source of revenue for the maintenance of the government, but when things get so out of hand that it is legally possible for the tax collector (that he has recently become a "director" doesn't make him any the less odious) to take away from a citizen as much as ninety percent of his income, surely history is waving a red lantern in front of us. Unless we slow down we may crash financially and go the way of those nations and empires of yesterday which have left only their crumbling ruins to bear testimony to their departed glory.

What then shall we do? As Christians, pay our taxes exactly as commanded us in the Word of God. As citizens of a democratic country, do whatever we in conscience believe will improve the quality of our leadership and postpone as long as possible the inevitable disaster. And above all things let "supplications, prayers, intercessions, and giving of thanks, be made for all men; For kings, and for all that are in authority; that we may lead a quiet and peaceable life in all godliness and honesty" (1 Timothy 2:1-2).

The Law of the Leader

Cattle are driven; sheep are led; and our Lord compares His people to sheep, not to cattle. It is especially important that Christian ministers know the law of the leader—that he can lead others only as far as he himself has gone. It is of course physically impossible for a shepherd to lead sheep unless he is ahead of them. To attempt to get them into pastures where he has not first gone he could only try to drive them, which would be to confuse them with cattle and to lose his own character as a true shepherd.

The minister must experience what he would teach or he will find himself in the impossible position of trying to drive sheep. For this reason he should seek to cultivate his own heart before he attempts to preach to the hearts of others. If his idea of the green pastures is a lush knowledge of

Bible doctrine, he can by hard study and careful teaching lead others as far as he has gone, viz., into a knowledge of doctrine. If he tries to bring them into a heart knowledge of truth which he has not actually experienced he will surely fail. In his frustration he may attempt to drive them; and scarcely anything is so disheartening as the sight of a vexed and confused shepherd using the lash on his bewildered flock in a vain attempt to persuade them to go on beyond the point to which he himself has attained.

There is of course a body of truth that cannot be experienced. By its very nature it can only be received and believed. Such, for instance, is the history recorded in the Bible and all prophetic Scripture yet unfulfilled. There is no way for these truths to be entered into except as we believe them as part of the total redemptive revelations. There is another vast body of truth which can have no final meaning for us except as we experience it. Grace, mercy, forgiveness, cleansing, personal faith in Christ, obedience, cross-carrying, death of the self-life, the infilling with the Holy Spirit, the indwelling of Christ and the walk in the Spirit: these are not doctrines to be believed merely, but spiritual experiences which a given man or woman may or may not enter into personally. These are the truths into which men cannot be driven, but only led by someone who has been there himself.

This law of the leader is demonstrated first in the life of our Lord. He did not and does not drive

His people; rather He leads the way Himself and enables His followers to come after Him. He suffered at the hands of men and can therefore fairly ask His people to suffer as He did. While He lived on earth He went about doing good, walking in dignified poverty, and it is no injustice when He calls His followers to lives of frugality and simplicity. He lived in the bosom of the Father even while here below (John 1:18), and led the way for us so we may do the same. He bore His cross and died upon it, so the New Testament requirement of personal crucifixion for all believers is morally logical. Finally, He arose and ascended to sit in heavenly places and thus give foundation to Paul's words in Colossians: "If ye then be risen with Christ, seek those things which are above, where Christ sitteth on the right hand of God. Set your affection on things above, not on things on the earth. For ye are dead, and your life is hid with Christ in God" (3:1-3).

The law of the leader tells us who are preachers that it is better to cultivate our souls than our voices. It is better to polish our hearts than our pulpit manners, though if the first has been done well and successfully it may be profitable for us to do the second. We cannot take our people beyond where we ourselves have been, and it thus becomes vitally important that we be men of God in the last and highest sense of that term.

What is true for preachers holds true for every Christian witness. Every writer, editor, Sunday school worker, singer, board member and deacon is bound by the law of the leader. He cannot lead where he has not been. Failure in his own life can only mean loss for those who look to him for leadership. Is that why James wrote, "My brethren, be not many masters, knowing that we shall receive the greater condemnation" (3:1)? It could be.

Other Titles by A.W. Tozer:

The following titles are also available as audio CDs, unabridged editions: